Reflections on Priestly Life

In the Footsteps of St. John Vianney,
the Curé of Ars

EDITED BY LEONARDO SAPIENZA

Libreria Editrice Vaticana

United States Conference of Catholic Bishops
Washington, DC

Contents

Introduction

It has been said that "style is the mark of what one is in what one does" (René Dumal). In the past, they used to say that "style makes the man." And it is true. In our behavior, our language, and our actions, we reveal our most intimate identity. Of course, we cannot base our assessment of a person on these aspects alone, because hypocrisy is often a cloudy, misleading smokescreen.

It is nonetheless inevitable: we show who we are through our words and actions. We need to remember that we have to *be* before we can *appear*, and not the other way around. If this is true for everyone, then it is even more true for a priest, whose chosen *style* of living is to be a model for the flock entrusted to him. As the words from one of the formulas of the Rite of Ordination state, your task as a priest is to "know what you do, imitate what you celebrate, and conform your life to the mystery of the Lord's Cross."

The style of *priestly life* is all right here.

The task of priests is to give the Lord: in the Eucharist, in word, and in charity. What a responsibility! That is why a priest needs to have a style of life conformed to this vocation: a style of living, a moral discipline, and a certain perfection. It is a lifestyle that is not always easy; it is a demanding and at times even inconvenient style of living that is not always fashionable. Yet it is precisely through this style of living that a priest finds his highest and fullest form of expression.

An elderly priest writes the following words with a certain sorrow: "The priestly lifestyle is fading because our intelligence is fading. . . . Every day I become more convinced that intelligence constitutes an irreplaceable element of a respectable and masculine priestly style of life."

May the Lord therefore help all priests to impress a gentle and austere *new style* upon our modern society, a lifestyle that demands and engenders holiness. It is a style of living that has been embodied by a great number of holy priests.

In order to recall those demands, the Holy Father Benedict XVI inaugurated a Year for Priests. To help us experience this moment of particular grace for priests, this book provides some of the written teachings of John XXIII, Paul VI, John Paul II, and the Holy Curé of Ars, whom the Pope wishes to proclaim the patron saint of all priests.

May the loving meditations of these pages awaken within priests a pride in their vocation, and awaken within the laity an affection for these brothers of theirs who, despite their many weaknesses, struggle to be *God's specialists* in the world.

Following the example of St. John Mary Vianney, may priests be able to respond to the strict demands of the life they have embraced. May they be faithful, generous, and glad; may they be living lenses of the great light that permeates them through the charism of Holy Orders.

And let us keep in mind that "in truly important matters, style matters most."

Leonardo Sapienza

The Firstfruits of Our Priesthood

The year 1959 was the centennial of the death of the Holy Curé of Ars. On the occasion of the fifty-fifth anniversary of his own priestly ordination, Pope John XXIII wrote the encyclical letter *Sacerdotii Nostri Primordia* in remembrance of the date, in order to highlight various aspects of priestly life and to present a successful model priest for all priests throughout the world.

To our Venerable Brethren, the Patriarchs, Primates, Archbishops, Bishops, and other Local Ordinaries in Peace and Communion with the Apostolic See.

Venerable Brethren, Health and Apostolic Benediction.

INTRODUCTION

1. When we think of the first days of our priesthood, which were so full of joyous consolations, we are reminded of one event that moved us to the very depths of our soul: the sacred ceremonies that were carried out so majestically in the Basilica of St. Peter's on January 8, 1905, when John Mary Baptist Vianney, a very humble French priest, was enrolled in the lists of the Blessed in Heaven. Our own ordination to the priesthood had taken place a few short months before, and it filled us with wonder to see the delight of our predecessor of happy memory, St. Pius X (who had once been the parish priest of the town of Salzano), as he offered this wonderful model of priestly virtues to all those entrusted with the care of souls,

Pope John XXIII, *Sacerdotii Nostri Primordia* (August 1, 1959), *www.vatican.va/holy_father/john_xxiii/encyclicals/documents/hf_j-xxiii_enc_19590801_sacerdotii_en.html.*

for their imitation. Now as we look back over the span of so many years, we never stop giving thanks to our Redeemer for this wonderful blessing, which marked the beginning of our priestly ministry and served as an effective heavenly incentive to virtue.

2. It is all the easier to remember, because on the very same day on which the honors of the Blessed were attributed to this holy man, word reached us of the elevation of that wonderful prelate, Giacomo M. Radini-Tedeschi, to the dignity of Bishop; a few days later, he was to call us to assist him in his work, and we found him a most loving teacher and guide. It was in his company that, early in 1905, we made our first pious pilgrimage to the tiny village called Ars, that had become so famous because of the holiness of its Curé.

3. Again, we cannot help thinking that it was through a special design of God's providence that the year in which we became a Bishop—1925—was the very one in which, toward the end of May, the Supreme Pontiff of happy memory, Pius XI, accorded the honors of sainthood to the humble Curé of Ars. In his talk on that occasion, the Supreme Pontiff chose to remind everyone of "the gaunt figure of John Baptist Vianncy, with that head shining with long hair that resembled a snowy crown, and that thin face, wasted from long fasting, where the innocence and holiness of the meekest and humblest of souls shone forth so clearly that the first sight of it called crowds of people back to thoughts of salvation."[1] A short while after, this same predecessor of ours took the occasion of the fiftieth anniversary of his own ordination to the priesthood to designate St. John Mary Vianney (to whose patronage St. Pius X had previously committed all of the shepherds of souls in France) as the heavenly patron of all "pastors, to promote their spiritual welfare throughout the world."[2]

A Time for Tribute
4. We have thought it opportune to use an Encyclical Letter to recall these acts of our Predecessors that are so closely bound up with such happy memories, Venerable Brethren, now that we are approaching the 100th anniversary of the day—August 4, 1859—on which this holy man, completely broken from forty years of the most tireless and exhausting labors, and already famous in every corner of the world for his holiness, passed on most piously to his heavenly reward.

5. And so we give thanks to God in His goodness, not only for seeing to it that this Saint would twice cast the brilliant light of his holiness over our priestly life at moments of great importance, but also for offering us an opportunity here at the beginning of our Pontificate to pay solemn tribute to this wonderful shepherd of souls on this happy 100th anniversary. It will be easy for you to see, Venerable Brethren, that we are directing this letter principally to our very dearest sons, those in sacred orders, and urging each and every one of them—especially those engaged in pastoral ministry—to devote all their attention to a consideration of the wonderful example of this holy man, who once shared in this priestly work and who now serves as their heavenly patron.

Earlier Popes on the Priesthood

6. The Supreme Pontiffs have issued many documents reminding those in sacred orders of the greatness of their priestly office, and pointing out the safest and surest way for them to carry out their duties properly. To recall only the more recent and more important of these, we would like to make special mention of the Apostolic Exhortation of St. Pius X of happy memory entitled *Haerent Animo*,[3] issued early in our priesthood, which urged us on to greater efforts to achieve a more ardent devotion, and the wonderful encyclical of our predecessor of happy memory, Pius XI, that began with the words *"ad catholici sacerdotii,"*[4] and finally the Apostolic Exhortation *Menti Nostrae*[5] of our immediate predecessor, along with his three allocutions on the occasion of the canonization of St. Pius X that give so clear and complete a picture of sacred orders.[6] Undoubtedly you are familiar with all of these documents, Venerable Brethren. But permit us also to mention a few words from a sermon published after the death of our immediate predecessor; they stand as the final solemn exhortation of that great Pontiff to priestly holiness: "Through the character of Sacred Orders, God willed to ratify that eternal covenant of love, by which He loves His priests above all others; and they are obliged to repay God for this special love with holiness of life. . . . So a cleric should be considered as a man chosen and set apart from the midst of the people, and blessed in a very special way with heavenly gifts—a sharer in divine power, and, to put it briefly, another Christ. . . . He is no longer supposed to live for himself; nor can he devote himself to the interests of just his own relatives, or friends or native land. . . . He must be aflame with charity toward

everyone. Not even his thoughts, his will, his feelings belong to him, for they are rather those of Jesus Christ who is his life."[7]

Subject of the Encyclical

7. St. John Mary Vianney is a person who attracts and practically pushes all of us to these heights of the priestly life. And so we are pleased to add our own exhortations to the others, in the hope that the priests of our day may exert every possible effort in this direction. We are well aware of their devoted care and interest, and well acquainted with the difficulties they face each day in their apostolic activity. And even though we regret the fact that the surging currents of this world overwhelm the spirit and courage of some and make them grow tired and inactive, we also know from experience how many more stand firm in their faith despite many hardships, and how many constantly strive to stir up an ardent zeal for the very highest ideals in their own souls. And yet, when they became priests, Christ the Lord spoke these words so full of consolation to all of them: "I no longer call you servants but friends."[8] May this encyclical of ours help the whole clergy to foster this divine friendship and grow in it, for it is the main source of the joy and the fruitfulness of any priestly work.

8. We have no intention, Venerable Brethren, of taking up each and every matter that has any reference to the life of a priest in the present day; as a matter of fact, following closely in the footsteps of St. Pius X, "we will not say anything that you have not already heard before, nor anything that will be completely new to anyone, but rather we will concentrate on recalling things that everyone ought to remember."[9] For a mere sketch of the qualities of this Heavenly soul, if done properly, is enough to lead us readily to a serious consideration of certain things that are, it is true, necessary in every age, but which now seem to be so important that our Apostolic office and duty force us to put special emphasis on them on the occasion of this centenary.

A Model for the Clergy

9. The Catholic Church, which elevated this man in sacred orders, who was "wonderful in his pastoral zeal, in his devotion to prayer and in the ardor of his penance"[10] to the honors of the saints of heaven, now, one hundred years after his death, offers him with maternal joy to all the

clergy as an outstanding model of priestly asceticism, of piety, especially in the form of devotion to the Eucharist, and, finally, of pastoral zeal.

PART I

10. You cannot begin to speak of St. John Mary Vianney without automatically calling to mind the picture of a priest who was outstanding in a unique way in voluntary affliction of his body; his only motives were the love of God and the desire for the salvation of the souls of his neighbors, and this led him to abstain almost completely from food and from sleep, to carry out the harshest kinds of penances, and to deny himself with great strength of soul. Of course, not all of the faithful are expected to adopt this kind of life; and yet divine providence has seen to it that there has never been a time when the Church did not have some pastors of souls of this kind who, under the inspiration of the Holy Spirit, did not hesitate for a moment to enter on this path, most of all because this way of life is particularly successful in bringing many men who have been drawn away by the allurement of error and vice back to the path of good living.

The Evangelical Counsels

11. The wonderful devotion in this regard of St. John Vianney—a man who was "hard on himself, and gentle with others"[11]—was so outstanding that it should serve as a clear and timely reminder of the important role that priests should attribute to the virtue of penance in striving for perfection in their own lives. Our predecessor of happy memory, Pius XII, in order to give a clear picture of this doctrine and to clear up the doubts and errors that bothered some people, denied that "the clerical state—as such, and on the basis of divine law—requires, of its very nature or at least as a result of some demand arising from its nature, that those enrolled in it observe the evangelical counsels,"[12] and justly concluded with these words: "Hence a cleric is not bound by virtue of divine law to the evangelical counsels of poverty, chastity, obedience."[13]

12. And yet it would undoubtedly be both a distortion of the real mind of this same Supreme Pontiff (who was so interested in the sanctity of the clergy) and a contradiction of the perpetual teaching of the Church in this matter, if anyone should dare to infer from this that clerics were any

less bound by their office than religious to strive for evangelical perfection of life. The truth is just the opposite; for the proper exercise of the priestly functions "requires a greater interior holiness than is demanded by the religious state."[14] And even if churchmen are not commanded to embrace these evangelical counsels by virtue of their clerical state, it still remains true that in their efforts to achieve holiness, these counsels offer them and all of the faithful the surest road to the desired goal of Christian perfection. What a great consolation it is to us to realize that at the present time many generous hearted priests are showing that they realize this; even though they belong to the diocesan clergy, they have sought the help and aid of certain pious societies approved by Church authorities in order to find a quicker and easier way to move along the road to perfection.

13. Fully convinced as they are that the "highest dignity of the priesthood consists in the imitation of Christ,"[15] churchmen must pay special attention to this warning of their Divine Master: "Whoever wishes to come after me must deny himself, take up his cross, and follow me."[16] It is recorded that "the holy parish priest of Ars often thought these words of the Lord over carefully, and determined to apply them to his own actions."[17] He made the resolution readily, and with the help of God's grace and by constant effort, he kept it to a wonderful extent; his example in the various works of priestly asceticism still points out the safest path to follow, and in the midst of this example, his poverty, chastity and obedience stand forth in a brilliant light.

The Poverty of St. John Vianney

14. First of all, you have clear testimony of his poverty. The humble Curé of Ars was careful to imitate the Patriarch of Assisi in this regard, for he had accepted his rule in the Third Order of St. Francis and he carefully observed it.[18] He was rich in his generosity toward others but the poorest of men in dealing with himself; he passed a life that was almost completely detached from the changeable, perishable goods of this world, and his spirit was free and unencumbered by impediments of this kind, so that it could always lie open to those who suffered from any kind of misery; and they flocked from everywhere to seek his consolation. "My secret," he said, "is easy to learn. It can be summed up in these few words: give everything away and keep nothing for yourself."[19]

15. This detachment from external goods enabled him to offer the most devoted and touching care to the poor, especially those in his own parish. He was very kind and gentle toward them and embraced them "with a sincere love, with the greatest of kindness, indeed with reverence."[20] He warned that the needy were never to be spurned since a disregard for them would reach in turn to God. When beggars knocked at his door, he received them with love and was very happy to be able to say to them: "I am living in need myself; I am one of you."[21] And toward the end of his life, he used to enjoy saying things like this: "I will be happy when I go; for now I no longer have any possessions; and so when God in his goodness sees fit to call me, I will be ready and willing to go."[22]

16. All of this will give you a clear idea of what we have in mind, Venerable Brethren, when we exhort all of our beloved sons who share in the priesthood to give careful thought to this example of poverty and charity. "Daily experience shows," wrote Pius XI, with St. John Mary Vianney specifically in mind, "that priests who live modestly and follow the teaching of the Gospel by paying little attention to their own interests, always confer wonderful benefits on the Christian people."[23] And the same Supreme Pontiff issued this serious warning to priests as well as to others in the course of a discussion of the current problems of society: "When they look around and see men ready to sell anything for money and to strike a bargain for anything at all, let them pass right through the midst of these attractions of vice without a thought or care for their own desires; and let them in their holiness spurn this base pursuit of wealth, and look for the riches of souls rather than for money, and let them long for and seek God's glory rather than their own."

The Use of Possessions

17. It is very important for these words to sink deep into the mind of every priest. If someone owns things that are rightfully his, let him be careful not to hang on to them greedily. Instead he should remember that the prescriptions of the *Code of Canon Law* dealing with church benefices make it clear that he has a serious obligation "to use superfluous income for the poor or for pious causes."[25] May God grant that no one of us ever lets that terrible sentence that the parish priest of Ars once used in rebuking his flock fall on him: "There are many people keeping their money hidden away while many others are dying of hunger."[26]

18. We know very well that at the present time there are many priests living in great need themselves. When they stop to realize that heavenly honors have been paid to one of their own who voluntarily gave up all he had and asked for nothing more than to be the poorest of all in his parish,[27] they have a wonderful source of inspiration for devoting themselves carefully and constantly to fostering evangelical poverty. And if our paternal interest can offer any consolation, we want them to know that we are very happy that they are serving Christ and the Church so generously with no thought of their own interests.

Unbecoming Indigence

19. However, even though we praise and extol this wonderful virtue of poverty so much, no one should conclude that we have any intention of giving our approval to the unbecoming indigence and misery in which the ministers of the Lord are sometimes forced to live, both in cities and in remote rural areas. In this regard, when St. Bede the Venerable explained and commented on the words of the Lord on detachment from earthly things, he excluded possible incorrect interpretations of this passage with these words: "You must not think that this command was given with the intention of having the saints keep no money at all for their own use or for that of the poor (for we read that the Lord himself . . . had money-boxes in forming his Church . . .) but rather the idea was that this should not be the motive for serving God nor should justice be abandoned out of fear of suffering want."[28] Besides, the laborer is worthy of his hire,[29] and we share the feelings of our immediate predecessor in urging the faithful to respond quickly and generously to the appeals of their pastors; we also join him in praising these shepherds for their efforts to see to it that those who help them in the sacred ministry do not lack the necessities of life.[30]

Model of Chastity

20. John M. Vianney was an outstanding model of voluntary mortification of the body as well as of detachment from external things. "There is only one way," he used to say, "for anyone to devote himself to God as he should through self-denial and the practice of penance: that is by devoting himself to it completely."[31] Throughout his whole life, the holy Curé of Ars carried this principle into practice energetically in the matter of chastity.

21. This wonderful example of chastity seems to have special application to the priests of our time who—as is unfortunately the case in many
regions—are often forced by the office they have assumed to live in the
midst of a human society that is infected by a general looseness in morals and a spirit of unbridled lust. How often this phrase of St. Thomas
Aquinas is proved true: "It is harder to lead a good life in the work of
caring for souls, because of the external dangers involved."[32] To this we
might add the fact that they often feel themselves cut off from the society
of others and that even the faithful to whose salvation they are dedicated do not understand them and offer them little help or support in
their undertakings.

22. We want to use this letter, Venerable Brethren, to exhort, again and
again, all of them, and especially those who are working alone and in the
midst of very serious dangers of this kind, to let their whole life, so to say,
resound with the splendor of holy chastity; St. Pius X had good reason to
call this virtue the "choicest adornment of our order."[33]

23. Venerable Brethren, do all you can and spare no effort to see to it that
the clergy entrusted to your care may enjoy living and working conditions
that will best foster and be of service to their ardent zeal. This means
that every effort should be exerted to eliminate the dangers that arise
from too great an isolation, to issue timely warnings against unwise or
imprudent actions, and last of all to check the dangers of idleness or of too
much external activity. In this regard, you should recall the wise directives
issued by our immediate Predecessor in the Encyclical *Sacra Virginitas*.[34]

St. John Vianney on Chastity

24. It is said that the face of the Pastor of Ars shone with an angelic
purity.[35] And even now anyone who turns toward him in mind and spirit
cannot help being struck, not merely by the great strength of soul with
which this athlete of Christ reduced his body to slavery,[36] but also by the
great persuasive powers he exercised over the pious crowds of pilgrims
who came to him and were drawn by his heavenly meekness to follow
in his footsteps. From his daily experiences in the Sacrament of Penance
he got an unmistakable picture of the terrible havoc that is wrought by
impure desire. This was what brought cries like these bursting from his
breast: "If there were not very innocent souls to please God and make up

for our offenses, how many terrible punishments we would have to suffer!" His own observations in this regard led him to offer this encouragement and advice to his hearers: "The works of penance abound in such delights and joys that once they have been tasted, nothing will ever again root them out of the soul. . . . Only the first steps are difficult for those who eagerly choose this path."[37]

Priest's Chastity as Help to Others

25. The ascetic way of life, by which priestly chastity is preserved, does not enclose the priest's soul within the sterile confines of his own interests, but rather it makes him more eager and ready to relieve the needs of his brethren. St. John Mary Vianney has this pertinent comment to make in this regard: "A soul adorned with the virtue of chastity cannot help loving others; for it has discovered the source and font of love—God." What great benefits are conferred on human society by men like this who are free of the cares of the world and totally dedicated to the divine ministry so that they can employ their lives, thoughts, powers in the interest of their brethren! How valuable to the Church are priests who are anxious to preserve perfect chastity! For we agree with our predecessor of happy memory, Pius XI, in regarding this as the outstanding adornment of the Catholic priesthood and as something "that seems to us to correspond better to the counsels and wishes of the Most Sacred Heart of Jesus, so far as the souls of priests are concerned."[38] Was not the mind of John Mary Vianney soaring to reach the counsels of this same divine charity when he wrote this lofty sentence: "Is the priesthood love of the Most Sacred Heart of Jesus?"[39]

The Obedience of St. John Vianney

27. There are many pieces of evidence of how this man was also outstanding in the virtue of obedience. It would be true to say that the fidelity toward his superiors in the Church which he pledged at the time he became a priest and which he preserved unshaken throughout his life drove him to an uninterrupted immolation of his will for forty years.

28. All his life he longed to lead a quiet and retired life in the background, and he regarded pastoral duties as a very heavy burden laid on his shoulders and more than once he tried to free himself of it. His obedience to his bishop was admirable; we would like to mention a few instances

of it in this encyclical, Venerable Brethren: "From the age of fifteen on, he ardently desired a solitary life, and as long as this wish was not fulfilled, he felt cut off from every advantage and every consolation that his state of life might have offered";[40] but "God never allowed this aim to be achieved. Undoubtedly, this was God's way of bending St. John Mary Vianney's will to obedience and of teaching him to put the duties of his office before his own desires; and so there was never a time when his devotion to self-denial did not shine forth";[41] "Out of complete obedience to his superiors, John M. Vianney carried out his tasks as pastor of Ars, and remained in that office till the end of his mortal life."[42]

29. It should be noted, however, that this full obedience of his to the commands of his superiors rested on supernatural principles; in acknowledging and duly obeying ecclesiastical authority, he was paying the homage of faith to the words of Christ the Lord as He told His Apostles, "He who hears you, hears me."[43] To conform himself faithfully to the will of his superiors he habitually restrained his own will, whether in accepting the holy burdens of hearing Confessions, or in performing zealously for his colleagues in the apostolate such work as would produce richer and more saving fruits.

The Importance of Obedience
30. We are offering clerics this total obedience as a model, with full confidence that its force and beauty will lead them to strive for it more ardently. And if there should be someone who dares to cast doubt on the supreme importance of this virtue—as sometimes happens at the present time— let him take to heart these words of our predecessor of happy memory, Pius XII, which everyone should keep firmly in mind: "The holiness of any life and the effectiveness of any apostolate has constant and faithful obedience to the hierarchy as its solid foundation, basis and support."[44]

31. For, as you well know, Venerable Brethren, our most recent predecessors have often issued serious warnings to priests about the extent of the dangers that are arising among the clergy from a growing carelessness about obedience with regard to the teaching authority of the Church, to the various ways and means of undertaking the apostolate, and to ecclesiastical discipline.

An Exhortation to Obedience

32. We do not want to spend a lot of time on this, but we think it timely to exhort all of our sons who share in the Catholic priesthood to foster a love in their souls that will make them feel attached to Mother Church by ever closer bonds, and then to make that love grow.

33. It is said that St. John M. Vianney lived in the Church in such a way that he worked for it alone, and burned himself up like a piece of straw being consumed on fiery coals. May that flame which comes from the Holy Spirit reach those of us who have been raised to the priesthood of Jesus Christ and consume us too.

34. We owe ourselves and all we have to the Church; may we work each day only in her name and by her authority and may we properly carry out the duties committed to us, and may we be joined together in fraternal unity and thus strive to serve her in that perfect way in which she ought to be served.[45]

Part II

35. St. John M. Vianney, who, as we have said, was so devoted to the virtue of penance, was just as sure that "a priest must be specially devoted to constant prayer."[46] In this regard, we know that shortly after he was made pastor of a village where Christian life had been languished for a long time, he began to spend long and happy hours at night (when he might have been resting) in adoration of Jesus in the Sacrament of His love. The Sacred Tabernacle seemed to be the spring from which he constantly drew the power that nourished his own piety and gave new life to it and promoted the effectiveness of his apostolic labor to such an extent that the wonderful words that our predecessor of happy memory, Pius XII, used to describe the ideal Christian parish, might well have been applied to the town of Ars in the time of this holy man: "In the middle stands the temple; in the middle of the temple the Sacred Tabernacle, and on either side the confessionals where supernatural life and health are restored to the Christian people."[47]

Prayer in the Life of St. John Vianney

36. How timely and how profitable this example of constant prayer on the part of a man completely dedicated to caring for the needs of souls is for priests in our own day, who are likely to attribute too much to the effectiveness of external activity and stand ready and eager to immerse themselves in the hustle and bustle of the ministry, to their own spiritual detriment!

37. "The thing that keeps us priests from gaining sanctity," the Curé of Ars used to say, "is thoughtlessness. It annoys us to turn our minds away from external affairs; we don't know what we really ought to do. What we need is deep reflection, together with prayer and an intimate union with God." The testimony of his life makes it clear that he always remained devoted to his prayers and that not even the duty of hearing confessions or any other pastoral office could cause him to neglect them. "Even in the midst of tremendous labors, he never let up on his conversation with God."[48]

38. But listen to his own words; for he seemed to have an inexhaustible supply of them whenever he talked about the happiness or the advantages that he found in prayer: "We are beggars who must ask God for everything";[49] "How many people we can call back to God by our prayers!"[50] And he used to say over and over again: "Ardent prayer addressed to God: this is man's greatest happiness on earth!"[51]

39. And he enjoyed this happiness abundantly when his mind rose with the help of heavenly light to contemplate the things of heaven and his pure and simple soul rose with all its deepest love from the mystery of the Incarnation to the heights of the Most Holy Trinity. And the crowds of pilgrims who surrounded him in the temple could feel something coming forth from the depths of the inner life of this humble priest when words like these burst forth from his inflamed breast, as they often did: "To be loved by God, to be joined to God, to walk before God, to live for God: O blessed life, O blessed death!"[52]

Necessity of Prayer Life

40. We sincerely hope, Venerable Brethren, that these lessons from the life of St. John M. Vianney may make all of the sacred ministers committed

to your care feel sure that they must exert every effort to be outstanding in their devotion to prayer; this can really be done, even if they are very busy with apostolic labors.

41. But if they are to do this, their lives must conform to the norms of faith that so imbued John Mary Vianney and enabled him to perform such wonderful works. "Oh the wonderful faith of this priest," one of his colleagues in the sacred ministry remarked. "It is great enough to enrich all the souls of the diocese!"[53]

42. This constant union with God is best achieved and preserved through the various practices of priestly piety; many of the more important of them, such as daily meditation, visits to the Blessed Sacrament, recitation of the Rosary, careful examination of conscience, the Church, in her wise and provident regulations, has made obligatory for priests.[54] As for the hours of the Office, priests have undertaken a serious obligation to the Church to recite them.[55]

43. The neglect of some of these rules may often be the reason why certain churchmen are caught up in the whirl of external affairs, gradually lose their feeling for sacred things and finally fall into serious difficulties when they are shorn of all spiritual protection and enticed by the attractions of this earthly life. John Mary Vianney on the contrary "never neglected his own salvation, no matter how busy he may have been with that of others."[56]

44. To use the words of St. Pius X: "We are sure of this much . . . that a priest must be deeply devoted to the practice of prayer if he is to live up to his rank and fulfill his duties properly. . . . For a priest must be much more careful than others to obey the command of Christ: You must always pray. Paul was only reaffirming this when he advised, as he did so often: be constant in prayer, ever on the watch to give thanks; pray without ceasing."[57] And we are more than happy to adopt as our own the words that our immediate predecessor offered priests as their password at the very beginning of his pontificate: "Pray, more and more, and pray more intensely."[58]

St. John Vianney's Devotion to the Eucharist

45. The devotion to prayer of St. John M. Vianney, who was to spend almost the whole of the last thirty years of his life in Church caring for the crowds of penitents who flocked to him, had one special characteristic—it was specially directed toward the Eucharist.

46. It is almost unbelievable how ardent his devotion to Christ hidden beneath the veils of the Eucharist really was. "He is the one," he said, "Who has loved us so much; why shouldn't we love Him in return?"[59] He was devoted to the adorable Sacrament of the altar with a burning charity and his soul was drawn to the sacred Tabernacle by a heavenly force that could not be resisted.

47. This is how he taught his faithful to pray: "You do not need many words when you pray. We believe on faith that the good and gracious God is there in the tabernacle; we open our souls to Him; and feel happy that He allows us to come before Him; this is the best way to pray."[60] He did everything that there was to be done to stir up the reverence and love of the faithful for Christ hidden in the Sacrament of the Eucharist and to bring them to share in the riches of the divine Synaxis; the example of his devotion was ever before them. "To be convinced of this," witnesses tell us, "all that was necessary was to see him carrying out the sacred ceremonies or simply to see him genuflect when he passed the tabernacle."[61]

Benefits from Eucharistic Prayer

48. As our predecessor of immortal memory, Pius XII, has said, "The wonderful example of St. John Mary Vianney retains all of its force for our times."[62] For the lengthy prayer of a priest before the adorable Sacrament of the Altar has a dignity and an effectiveness that cannot be found elsewhere nor be replaced. And so when the priest adores Christ our Lord and gives thanks to Him, or offers satisfaction for his own sins and those of others, or finally when he prays constantly that God keep special watch over the causes committed to his care, he is inflamed with a more ardent love for the Divine Redeemer to whom he has sworn allegiance and for those to whom he is devoting his pastoral care. And a devotion to the Eucharist that is ardent, constant and that carries over into works also has the effect of nourishing and fostering the inner perfection of his soul and

assuring him, as he carries out his apostolic duties, of an abundance of the supernatural powers that the strongest workers for Christ must have.

49. We do not want to skip over the benefits that accrue to the faithful themselves in this way, as they see the piety of their priests and are drawn by their example. For, as our predecessor of happy memory, Pius XII, pointed out in a talk to the clergy of this dear city: "If you want the faithful who are entrusted to your care to pray willingly and well, you must give them an example and let them see you praying in church. A priest kneeling devoutly and reverently before the tabernacle, and pouring forth prayers to God with all his heart, is a wonderful example to the Christian people and serves as an inspiration."[63] The saintly Curé of Ars used all of these helps in carrying out his apostolic office, and without a doubt they are suitable to all times and places.

The Mass and the Priesthood

50. But never forget that the principal form of Eucharistic prayer is contained in the holy Sacrifice of the Altar. It is our opinion that this point ought to be considered more carefully, Venerable Brethren, for it touches on a particularly important aspect of priestly life.

51. It is not our intention at this time to enter upon a lengthy treatment of the Church's teaching on the priesthood and on the Eucharistic Sacrifice as it has been handed down from antiquity. Our predecessors Pius XI and Pius XII have done this in clear and important documents and we urge you to take pains to see to it that the priests and faithful entrusted to your care are very familiar with them. This will clear up the doubts of some; and correct the more daring statements that have sometimes been made in discussing these matters.

52. But we too hope to say something worthwhile in this matter by showing the principal reason why the holy Curé of Ars, who, as befits a hero, was most careful in fulfilling his priestly duties, really deserves to be proposed to those who have the care of souls as a model of outstanding virtue and to be honored by them as their heavenly patron. If it is obviously true that a priest receives his priesthood so as to serve at the altar and that he enters upon this office by offering the Eucharistic Sacrifice, then it is equally true that for as long as he lives as God's minister, the Eucharistic

Sacrifice will be the source and origin of the holiness that he attains and of the apostolic activity to which he devotes himself. All of these things came to pass in the fullest possible way in the case of St. John Vianney.

53. For, if you give careful consideration to all of the activity of a priest, what is the main point of his apostolate if not seeing to it that wherever the Church lives, a people who are joined by the bonds of faith, regenerated by holy Baptism and cleansed of their faults will be gathered together around the sacred altar? It is then that the priest, using the sacred power he has received, offers the divine Sacrifice in which Jesus Christ renews the unique immolation which He completed on Calvary for the redemption of mankind and for the glory of His heavenly Father. It is then that the Christians who have gathered together, acting through the ministry of the priest, present the divine Victim and offer themselves to the supreme and eternal God as a "sacrifice, living, holy, pleasing to God."[64] There it is that the people of God are taught the doctrines and precepts of faith and are nourished with the Body of Christ, and there it is that they find a means to gain supernatural life, to grow in it, and if need be to regain unity. And there besides, the Mystical Body of Christ, which is the Church, grows with spiritual increase throughout the world down to the end of time.

54. It is only right and fitting to call the life of St. John Vianney a priestly and pastoral one in an outstanding way, because he spent more and more time in preaching the truths of religion and cleansing souls of the stain of sin as the years went by, and because he was mindful of the altar of God in each and every act of his sacred ministry!

55. It is true of course that the holy Curé's fame made great crowds of sinners flock to Ars, while many priests experience great difficulty in getting the people committed to their care to come to them at all, and then find that they have to teach them the most elementary truths of Christian doctrine just as if they were working in a missionary land. But as important and sometimes as trying as these apostolic labors may be, they should never be permitted to make men of God forget the great importance of the goal which they must always keep in view and which St. John Vianney attained through dedicating himself completely to the main works of the apostolic life in a tiny country church.

Personal Holiness and the Mass

56. This should be kept in mind, in particular: whatever a priest may plan, resolve, or do to become holy, he will have to draw, for example and for heavenly strength, upon the Eucharistic Sacrifice which he offers, just as the Roman Pontifical urges: "Be aware of what you are doing; imitate what you hold in your hands."

57. In this regard, we are pleased to repeat the words used by our immediate predecessor of happy memory in the Apostolic Exhortation entitled *Menti Nostrae*: "Just as the whole life of our Savior was pointed toward His sacrifice of Himself, so too the life of the priest, who must reproduce the image of Christ in himself, must become a pleasing sacrifice with Him and through Him and in Him. . . . And so it is not enough for him to celebrate the Eucharistic sacrifice, but in a very deep sense, he must live it; for in this way, he can draw from it the heavenly strength that will enable him to be profoundly transformed and to share in the expiatory life of the Divine Redeemer himself. . . ."[65] And again: "The soul of the priest must refer what takes place on the sacrificial altar to himself; for just as Jesus Christ immolates Himself, his minister must immolate himself along with Him; just as Jesus expiates the sins of men, so too the priest must tread the lofty path of Christian asceticism to bring about his own purification and that of his neighbors."[66]

Safeguarding Holiness

58. This lofty aspect of doctrine is what the Church has in mind when, with maternal care, she invites her sacred ministers to devote themselves to asceticism and urges them to celebrate the Eucharistic Sacrifice with the greatest possible interior and exterior devotion. May not the fact that some priests fail to keep in mind the close connection that ought to exist between the offering of the Sacrifice and their own self-dedication be the reason why they gradually fall off from that first fervor they had at the time of their ordination? St. John Vianney learned this from experience and expressed it this way: "The reason why priests are remiss in their personal lives is that they do not offer the Sacrifice with attention and piety." And he, who in his lofty virtue was in the habit of "offering himself as an expiation for sinners,"[67] used to weep "when he thought of the unhappy priests who did not measure up to the holiness demanded by their office."[68]

59. Speaking as a Father, we urge our beloved priests to set aside a time to examine themselves on how they celebrate the divine mysteries, what their dispositions of soul and external attitude are as they ascend the altar and what fruit they are trying to gain from it. They should be spurred to do this by the centenary celebrations that are being held in honor of this outstanding and wonderful priest, who drew such great strength and such great desire to dedicate himself "from the consolation and happiness of offering the divine victim."[69] May his prayers, which we feel sure they will have, bring a fullness of light and strength down upon our beloved priests.

Part III

60. The wonderful examples of priestly asceticism and prayer that we have proposed for your consideration up to now, Venerable Brethren, also point clearly to the source of the pastoral skill and of the truly remarkable heavenly effectiveness of the sacred ministry of St. John M. Vianney. In this regard, our predecessor of happy memory, Pius XII, gave a wise warning: "The priest should realize that the important ministry entrusted to him will be more fruitfully carried out, the more intimately he is united with Christ and led on by His spirit."[70] As a matter of fact, the life of the Curé of Ars offers one more outstanding argument in support of the supreme rule for apostolic labor that was laid down by Jesus Christ Himself: "Without me, you can do nothing."[71]

The Good Shepherd
61. We have no intention of trying to make a list of all the wonderful things done by this humble Curé of a country parish, who drew such immense crowds to the tribunal of Penance that some people, out of contempt, called him "a kind of nineteenth-century rabble-rouser";[72] nor do we see any need of going into all of the particular ways in which he carried out his duties, some of which, perhaps, could not be accommodated to our times.

62. But we do want to recall this one fact—that this Saint was in his own times a model of pastoral devotion in a tiny community that was still suffering from the loss of Christian faith and morals that occurred while the French Revolution was raging. This was the mission and command

received just before taking over his pastoral office: "You will not find love of God in that parish; stir it up yourself."[73]

63. He proved to be a tireless worker for God, one who was wise and devoted in winning over young people and bringing families back to the standards of Christian morality, a shepherd who was never too tired to show an interest in the human needs of his flock, one whose own way of life was very close to theirs and who was prepared to exert every effort and make any sacrifice to establish Christian schools and to make missions available to the people: and all of these things show that St. John M. Vianney reproduced the true image of the good shepherd in himself as he dealt with the flock entrusted to his care, for he knew his sheep, protected them from dangers, and gently but firmly looked after them.

64. Without realizing it, he was sounding his own praises in the words he once addressed to his people: "Good shepherd! O shepherd who lives up to the commands and desires of Jesus Christ completely! This is the greatest blessing that a kind and gracious God can send to a parish."[74]

65. But there are three things in particular of lasting value and importance that the example of this holy man brings home to us and it is to these in particular that we would like to direct your attention, Venerable Brethren.

His Esteem for the Pastoral Office

66. The first thing that strikes us is the very high esteem in which he held his pastoral office. He was so humble by disposition and so much aware through faith of the importance of the salvation of a human soul that he could never undertake his parish duties without a feeling of fear.

67. "My friend," these are the words he used to open his heart to a fellow-priest, "you have no idea of how fearful a thing it is for a priest to be snatched away from the care of souls to appear before the judgment seat of God."[75]

68. Everyone knows—as we have already pointed out—how much he yearned and how long he prayed to be allowed to go off by himself to weep and to make proper expiation for what he called his miserable life; and we also know that only obedience and his zeal for the salvation of others got him to return to the field of the apostolate when he had abandoned it.

Sufferings for His Sheep

69. But if he felt the great weight of this burden to be so heavy that it sometimes seemed to be crushing him, this was also the reason why he conceived his office and its duties in so lofty a fashion that carrying them out called for great strength of soul. These are the prayers he addressed to heaven as he began his parochial ministry: "My God, make the sheep entrusted to me come back to a good way of life. For all my life I am prepared to endure anything that pleases you."[76]

70. And God heard these fervent prayers, for later our saint had to confess: "If I had known when I came to the parish of Ars what I would have to suffer, the fear of it would certainly have killed me."[77]

71. Following in the footsteps of the great apostles of all ages, he knew that the best and most effective way for him to contribute to the salvation of those who would be entrusted to his care was through the cross. It was for them that he put up with all sorts of calumnies, prejudices and opposition, without complaint; for them that he willingly endured the sharp discomforts and annoyances of mind and body that were forced upon him by his daily administration of the Sacrament of Penance for thirty years with almost no interruption; for them that this athlete of Christ fought off the powers of hell; for them, last of all, that he brought his body into subjection through voluntary mortification.

72. Almost everyone knows his answer to the priest who complained to him that his apostolic zeal was bearing no fruit: "You have offered humble prayers to God, you have wept, you have groaned, you have sighed. Have you added fasts, vigils, sleeping on the floor, castigation of your body? Until you have done all of these, do not think that you have tried everything."[78]

Need for Comparison

73. Once again our mind turns to sacred ministers who have the care of souls, and we urgently beg them to realize the importance of these words. Let each one think over his own life, in the light of the supernatural prudence that should govern all of our actions, and ask himself if it is really all that the pastoral care of the people entrusted to him requires.

74. With firm confidence that the merciful God will never fail to offer the help that human weakness calls for, let sacred ministers think over the

offices and burdens they have assumed by looking at St. John M. Vianney as if he were a mirror. "A terrible disaster strikes us curés," the holy man complained, "when our spirit grows lazy and careless"; he was referring to the harmful attitude of those pastors who are not disturbed by the fact that many sheep committed to them are growing filthy in the slavery of sin. If they want to imitate the Curé of Ars more closely, who was so "convinced that men should be loved, so that we can do good to them,"[79] then let these priests ask themselves what kind of love they have for those whom God has entrusted to their care and for whom Christ has died!

75. Because of human liberty and of events beyond all human control, the efforts of even the holiest of men will sometimes fail. But a priest ought to remember that in the mysterious counsels of Divine Providence, the eternal fate of many men is bound up with his pastoral interest and care and the example of his priestly life. Is not this thought powerful enough both to stir up the lackadaisical in an effective way and to urge on to greater efforts those who are already zealous in the work of Christ?

Preacher and Catechist

76. Because, as is recorded, "he was always ready to care for the needs of souls,"[80] St. John M. Vianney, good shepherd that he was, was also outstanding in offering his sheep an abundant supply of the food of Christian truth. Throughout his life, he preached and taught Catechism.

77. The Council of Trent pronounced this to be a parish priest's first and greatest duty and everyone knows what immense and constant labor John Vianney expended in order to be equal to carrying out this task. For he began his course of studies when he was already along in years, and he had great difficulty with it; and his first sermons to the people kept him up for whole nights on end. How much the ministers of the word of God can find here to imitate! For there are some who give up all effort at further study and then point too readily to his small fund of learning as an adequate excuse for themselves. They would be much better off if they would imitate the great perseverance of soul with which the Curé of Ars prepared himself to carry out this great ministry to the best of his abilities: which, as a matter of fact, were not quite as limited as is sometimes believed, for he had a clear mind and sound judgment.[81]

Obligation to Learn

78. Men in Sacred Orders should gain an adequate knowledge of human affairs and a thorough knowledge of sacred doctrine that is in keeping with their abilities. Would that all pastors of souls would exert as much effort as the Curé of Ars did to overcome difficulties and obstacles in learning, to strengthen memory through practice, and especially to draw knowledge from the Cross of our Lord, which is the greatest of all books. This is why his Bishop made this reply to some of his critics: "I do not know whether he is learned; but a heavenly light shines in him."[82]

Model for Preachers

79. This is why our predecessor of happy memory, Pius XII, was perfectly right in not hesitating to offer this country curé as a model for the preachers of the Holy City: "The holy Curé of Ars had none of the natural gifts of a speaker that stand out in men like P. Segneri or B. Bossuet. But the clear, lofty, living thoughts of his mind were reflected in the sound of his voice and shone forth from his glance, and they came out in the form of ideas and images that were so apt and so well fitted to the thoughts and feelings of his listeners and so full of wit and charm that even St. Francis de Sales would have been struck with admiration. This is the kind of speaker who wins the souls of the faithful. A man who is filled with Christ will not find it hard to discover ways and means of bringing others to Christ."[83]

80. These words give a wonderful picture of the Curé of Ars as a catechism teacher and as a preacher. And when, towards the end of his life on earth, his voice was too weak to carry to his listeners, the sparkle and gleam of his eyes, his tears, his sighs of divine love, the bitter sorrow he evidenced when the mere concept of sin came to his mind, were enough to convert to a better way of life the faithful who surrounded his pulpit. How could anyone help being moved deeply with a life so completely dedicated to Christ shining so clearly there before him?

81. Up to the time of his blessed death, St. John M Vianney held on tenaciously to his office of teaching the faithful committed to his care and the pious pilgrims who crowded the church, by denouncing evil of every kind, in whatever guise it might appear, "in season, out of season,"[84] and, even more, by sublimely raising souls to God; for "he preferred to show the beauties of virtue rather than the ugliness of vice."[85] For this humble priest

understood perfectly how great the dignity and sublimity of teaching the word of God really is. "Our Lord," he said, "who Himself is truth, has as much regard for His word as for His Body."

The Obligation to Teach

82. So it is easy to realize what great joy it brought our predecessors to point out an example like this to be imitated by those who guide the Christian people; for the proper and careful exercise of the teaching office by the clergy is of great importance. In speaking of this, St. Pius X had this to say: "We want especially to pursue this one point and to urge strongly that no priest has any more important duty or is bound by any stricter obligation."[86]

83. And so once again we take this warning which our predecessors have repeated over and over again and which has been inserted in the *Code of Canon Law* as well,[87] and we issue it to you, Venerable Brethren, on the occasion of the solemn celebration of the centenary of the holy catechist and preacher of Ars.

84. In this regard we wish to offer our praise and encouragement to the studies that have been carefully and prudently carried on in many areas under your leadership and auspices, to improve the religious training of both youngsters and adults by presenting it in a variety of forms that are specially adapted to local circumstances and needs. All of these efforts are useful; but on the occasion of this centenary, God wants to cast new light on the wonderful power of the apostolic spirit, that sweeps all in its path, as it is exemplified in this priest who throughout his life was a witness in word and deed for Christ nailed to the cross "not in the persuasive language devised by human wisdom, but in a manifestation of spiritual power."[88]

His Ministry in the Confessional

85. All that remains for us to do is to recall at a little greater length the pastoral ministry of St. John M. Vianney, which was a kind of steady martyrdom for a long period of his life, and especially his administration of the Sacrament of Penance, which calls for special praise for it brought forth the richest and most salutary fruits.

86. "For almost fifteen hours each day, he lent a patient ear to penitents. This work began early in the morning and continued well on into the night."[89] And when he was completely worn out and broken five days before his death and had no strength left, the final penitents came to his bed. Toward the end of his life, the number of those who came to see him each year reached eighty thousand according to the accounts.[90]

His Anguish over Sins

87. It is hard to imagine what pain and discomfort and bodily sufferings this man underwent as he sat to hear Confessions in the tribunal of Penance for what seemed like endless periods of time, especially if you recall how weakened he was by his fasts, mortifications, sicknesses, vigils and lack of sleep.

88. But he was bothered even more by a spiritual anguish that took complete possession of him. Listen to his mournful cries: "So many crimes against God are committed," he said, "that they sometimes incline us to ask God to end this world! . . . You have to come to the town of Ars if you really want to learn what an infinite multitude of serious sins there are. . . . Alas, we do not know what to do, we think that there is nothing else to do than weep and pray to God."

89. And this holy man could have added that he had taken on himself more than his share of the expiation of these sins. For he told those who asked his advice in this regard: "I impose only a small penance on those who confess their sins properly; the rest I perform in their place."[91]

His Concern for Sinners

90. St. John M. Vianney always had "poor sinners," as he called them, in his mind and before his eyes, with the constant hope of seeing them turn back to God and weep for the sins they had committed. This was the object of all his thoughts and cares, and of the work that took up almost all his time and efforts.[92]

91. From his experience in the tribunal of Penance, in which he loosed the bonds of sin, he understood just how much malice there is in sin and what terrible devastation it wreaks in the souls of men. He used to paint

it in hideous colors: "If we," he asserted, "had the faith to see a soul in mortal sin, we would die of fright."[93]

92. But the sufferings of souls who have remained attached to their sins in hell did not add to the strength and vigor of his own sorrow and words as much as did the anguish he felt at the fact that divine love had been carelessly neglected or violated by some offense. This stubbornness in sin and ungrateful disregard for God's great goodness made rivers of tears flow from his eyes. "My friend," he said, "I am weeping because you are not."[94]

93. And yet, what great kindness he displayed in devoting himself to restoring hope to the souls of repentant sinners! He spared no effort to become a minister of divine mercy to them; and he described it as "like an overflowing river that carries all souls along with it"[95] and throbs with a love greater than that of a mother, "for God is quicker to forgive than a mother to snatch her child from the fire."[96]

The Seriousness of Confession

94. Let the example of the Curé of Ars stir up those who are in charge of souls to be eager and well-prepared in devoting themselves to this very serious work, for it is here most of all that divine mercy finally triumphs over human malice and that men have their sins wiped away and are reconciled to God.

95. And let them also remember that our predecessor of happy memory, Pius XII, expressed disapproval "in the strongest terms" of the opinion of those who have little use for frequent confession, where it is a matter of venial sins; the Supreme Pontiff said: "We particularly recommend the pious practice of frequent confession, which the Church has introduced, under the influence of the Holy Spirit, as a means of swifter daily progress along the road of virtue."[97]

96. Again, we have complete confidence that sacred ministers will be even more careful than others in faithfully observing the prescriptions of Canon Law,[98] which make the pious use of the Sacrament of Penance, which is so necessary for the attainment of sanctity, obligatory at certain specified times; and that they will treat those urgent exhortations which

this same predecessor of ours made "with a sorrowful soul" on several occasions[99] with the supreme veneration and obedience they deserve.

Necessity of Personal Holiness

97. As this Encyclical of ours draws to a close, we want to assure you, Venerable Brethren, of the high hopes we have that these centenary celebrations will, with the help of God, lead to a deeper desire and more intensive efforts on the part of all priests to carry out their sacred ministry with more ardent zeal and especially to work to fulfill "the first duty of priests, that is, the duty of becoming holy themselves."[100]

98. When we gaze from this height of the Supreme Pontificate to which we have been raised by the secret counsels of Divine Providence and turn our mind to what souls are hoping for and expecting, or to the many areas of the earth that have not yet been brightened by the light of the Gospel, or last of all to the many needs of the Christian people, the figure of the priest is always before our eyes.

99. If there were no priests or if they were not doing their daily work, what use would all these apostolic undertakings be, even those which seem best suited to the present age? Of what use would be the laymen who work so zealously and generously to help in the activities of the apostolate?

100. And so we do not hesitate to speak to all of these sacred ministers, whom we love so much and in whom the Church rests such great hopes— these priests—and urge them in the name of Jesus Christ from the depths of a father's heart to be faithful in doing and giving all that the seriousness of their ecclesiastical dignity requires of them.

101. This appeal of ours draws added force from the wise and prudent words of St. Pius X: "Nothing is needed more to promote the kingdom of Jesus Christ in the world than the holiness of churchmen, who should stand out above the faithful by their example, their words and their teaching."[101]

102. And this fits in perfectly with the words that St. John M. Vianney addressed to his bishop: "If you want the whole diocese to be converted to God, then all of the Curés must become holy."

Help from Bishops

103. And we especially want to commend these most beloved sons to you, Venerable Brethren, who bear the chief responsibility for the holiness of your clergy, so that you will be careful to go to them and help them in the difficulties—sometimes serious ones—that they face in their own lives or in carrying out their duties.

104. What is there that cannot be accomplished by a bishop who loves the clergy entrusted to his direction, who is close to them, really knows them, takes great care of them and directs them in a firm but fatherly way?

105. It is true that your pastoral care is supposed to extend to the whole diocese, but you should still take very special care of those who are in sacred orders, for they are your closest helpers in your work and are bound to you by many sacred ties.

Help from the Faithful

106. On the occasion of this centenary celebration, we would also like to exhort paternally all of the faithful to offer constant prayers to God for their priests, so that each in his own way may help them attain holiness.

107. Those who are more fervent and devout are turning their eyes and their minds to the priest with a great deal of hope and expectation. For, at a time when you find flourishing everywhere the power of money, the allure of pleasures of the senses, and too great an esteem for technical achievements, they want to see in him a man who speaks in the name of God, who is animated by a firm faith, and who gives no thought to himself, but burns with intense charity.

108. So let them all realize that they can help sacred ministers a great deal to achieve this lofty goal, if only they will show due respect for priestly dignity, and have proper esteem for their pastoral office and its difficulties, and finally be even more zealous and active in offering to help them.

A Call for Vocations

109. We cannot help turning our paternal spirit in a special way to young people; we embrace them with a warm love and remind them that, in them, the Church rests great hopes for the years to come.

110. The harvest indeed is great, but the laborers are few.[102] How many areas there are where the heralds of the Gospel truth are worn out by their labors and waiting eagerly and longingly for those to come who will take their place! There are peoples who are languishing in a miserable hunger for heavenly food more than for earthly nourishment. Who will bring the heavenly banquet of life and truth to them?

111. We have complete confidence that the youngsters of our time will be as quick as those of times past to give a generous answer to the invitation of the Divine Master to provide for this vital need.

112. Priests often find themselves in difficult circumstances. This is not surprising; for those who hate the Church always show their hostility by trying to harm and deceive her sacred ministers; as the Curé of Ars himself admitted, those who want to overthrow religion always try in their hatred to strike at priests first of all.

113. But even in the face of these serious difficulties, priests who are ardent in their devotion to God enjoy a real, sublime happiness from an awareness of their own position, for they know that they have been called by the Divine Savior to offer their help in a most holy work, which will have an effect on the redemption of the souls of men and on the growth of the Mystical Body of Christ. So let Christian families consider it one of their most sublime privileges to give priests to the Church; and so let them offer their sons to the sacred ministry with joy and gratitude.

Lourdes and Ars

114. There is no need to dwell on this point, Venerable Brothers, since what we are urging is very close to your own hearts. For we are sure that you understand perfectly our interest in these things and the forceful expression we are giving to it, and that you share it. For the present, we commit this matter of immense importance, closely bound up with the salvation of many souls, to the intercession of St. John M. Vianney.

115. We also turn our eyes to the Mother of God, immaculate from the very beginning. Shortly before the Curé of Ars, filled with heavenly merits, completed his long life, She appeared in another part of France to an innocent and humble girl, and through her, invited men with a mother's insistence to devote themselves to prayers and Christian penance; this

majestic voice is still striking home to souls a century later, and echoing far and wide almost endlessly.

116. The things that were done and said by this holy priest, who was raised to the honors of the Heavenly Saints and whose 100th anniversary we are commemorating, cast a kind of heavenly light beforehand over the supernatural truths which were made known to the innocent girl at the grotto of Lourdes. For this man had such great devotion to the Immaculate Conception of the Virgin Mother of God that in 1836 he dedicated his parish church to Mary Conceived Without Sin and greeted the infallible definition of this truth as Catholic dogma in 1854 with the greatest joy and reverence.[103]

117. So there is good reason for us to link together this double centenary, of Lourdes and of Ars, as we give proper thanks to the most high God: each supplements the other, and each does honor to a nation we love very much and which can boast of having both of these most holy places in its bosom.

118. Mindful of the many benefits that have been received, and trusting confidently that still more will come to us and to the whole Church, we borrow the prayer that sounded so often on the lips of the Curé of Ars: "Blessed be the most holy and immaculate conception of the Blessed Virgin Mary, Mother of God. May all nations praise, all lands invoke and preach your Immaculate Heart!"[104]

119. Confident that this centennial celebration of St. John M. Vianney throughout the world will stir up the pious zeal of priests and of those whom God is calling to take up the priesthood, and will make all the faithful even more active and interested in supplying the things that are needed for priests' life and work, with all our heart we impart the Apostolic Blessing to each and every one of them, and especially to you, Venerable Brethren, as a consoling pledge of heavenly graces and of our good will.

Given at Rome, at St. Peter's, on August 1, 1959, the first year of our Pontificate.

John XXIII

Notes

1   AAS 17 (1925) 224.
2   Apostolic letter *Anno Iubilari*, AAS 21 (1929) 313.
3   *Acta Pii* X, IV, pp. 237-264.
4   AAS 28 (1936) 5-53.
5   AAS 42 (1950) 657-702.
6   AAS 46 (1954) 313-317, 666-677; TPS v. l, no. 2, pp. 147-158.
7   Cf. AAS 50 (1958) 966-967.
8   *Pontificale Rom.*; cf. Jn 15:15.
9   Exhortation *Haerent animo*, *Acta Pii* X, IV, p. 238.
10   Prayer of the Mass on the feast of St. John Mary Vianney.
11   Cf. *Archiv. Secr. Vat.*, C.SS. Rituum, *Processus*, v. 227, p. 196.
12   Allocution *Annus sacer*, AAS 43 (1951) 29.
13   Ibid.
14   St. Thomas, *Summa Theologiae* II-II, q. 184, a. 8, in c.
15   Cf. Pius XII, Allocution, April 16, 1953: AAS 45 (1953) 288.
16   Mt 16:24.
17   Cf. *Archiv. Secret. Vat.*, v. 227, p. 42.
18   Cf. ibid., v. 227, p. 13i.
19   Cf. ibid., v. 227, p. 92.
20   Cf. ibid., v. 3897, p. 510.
21   Cf. ibid., v. 227, p. 334.
22   Cf. ibid., v. 227, p. 305.
23   Encyclical letter *Divini Redemptoris*, AAS 29 (1937) 99.
24   Encyclical letter *Ad catholici sacerdotii*, AAS 28 (1936) 28.
25   CIC, c. 1473.
26   Cf. *Sermons du B. Jean B. M. Vianney*, 1909, v. 1, p. 364.
27   Cf. *Archiv. Secret. Vat.*, v. 227, p. 91.
28   *In Lucae Evangelium Expositio*, IV, in c. 12; Migne, PL 92, col. 494-495.
29   Cf. Lk 10:7.
30   Cf. apostolic exhortation *Menti Nostrae*, AAS 42 (1950) 697-699.
31   Cf. *Archiv. Secret. Vat.*, v. 227, p. 91.
32   *Summa Theologiae* II-II, q. 184, a. 8, in c.
33   Exhortation *Haerent animo*; *Acta Pii* X, IV, p. 260.
34   AAS 46 (1954) 161-191; TPS (1954) v. 1, no. 1, pp. 101-123.
35   Cf. *Archiv. Secret. Vat.*, v. 3897, p. 536.
36   Cf. 1 Cor 9:27.
37   Cf. *Archiv. Secret. Vat.*, v. 3897, p. 304.
38   Encyclical letter *Ad catholici sacerdotii*, AAS 28 (1936) 28.
39   Cf. *Archiv. Secret Vat.*, v. 227, p. 29.
40   Cf. ibid., v. 227, p. 74.
41   Cf. ibid., v. 227, p. 39.
42   Cf. ibid., v. 3895, p. 153.

43   Lk 10:16.
44   Exhortation *In auspicando*, AAS 40 (1948) 375.
45   Cf. *Archiv. Secret. Vat.*, v. 227, p. 136.
46   Cf. ibid., v. 227, p. 33.
47   Cf. *Discorsi e radiomessaggi* di S.S. Pio XII, v. 14, p. 452.
48   Cf. *Archiv. Secret. Vat.*, v. 227, p. 131.
49   Cf. ibid., v. 227, p. 1100.
50   Cf. ibid., v. 227, p. 54.
51   Cf. ibid., v. 227, p. 45.
52   Cf. ibid., v. 227, p. 29.
53   Cf. ibid., v. 227, p. 976.
54   CIC, c. 125.
55   Ibid., c. 135.
56   Cf. *Archiv. Secret. Vat.*, v. 227, p. 36.
57   Exhortation *Haerent animo*, Acta Pii X, IV, pp. 248-249.
58   Discourse of June 24, 1939: AAS 31 (1939) 249.
59   Cf. *Archiv. Secret. Vat.*, v. 227, p. 1103.
60   Cf. ibid., v. 227, p. 45.
61   Cf. ibid., v. 227, p. 459.
62   Cf. Message of June 25, 1956: AAS 48 (1956) 579.
63   Cf. Discourse of March 13, 1943: AAS 35 (1943) 114-115.
64   Rom 12:1.
65   Apostolic exhortation *Menti Nostrae*, AAS 42 (1950) 666-667.
66   Cf. ibid., 667-668.
67   Cf. *Archiv. Secret. Vat.*, v. 227, p. 319.
68   Cf. ibid., v. 227, p. 47.
69   Cf. ibid., pp. 667-668.
70   Apostolic exhortation *Menti Nostrae*, AAS 42 (1950) 676.
71   Jn 15:5.
72   Cf. *Archiv. Secret. Vat.*, v. 227, p. 629.
73   Cf. ibid., v. 227, p. 15.
74   Cf. *Sermons*, 1.c., v. 2, p. 86.
75   Cf. *Archiv. Secret. Vat.*, v. 227, p. 1210.
76   Cf. *Archiv. Secret. Vat.*, v. 227, p. 53.
77   Cf. ibid., v. 227, p. 991.
78   Cf. ibid., v. 227, p. 53.
79   Cf. *Archiv. Secret. Vat.*, v. 227, p. 1002.
80   Cf. ibid., v. 227, p. 580.
81   Cf. *Archiv. Secret Vat.*, v. 3897, p. 444.
82   Cf. ibid., v. 3897, p. 272.
83   Cf. Discourse of March 16, 1946: AAS 38 (1946) 186.
84   2 Tm 4:2.
85   Cf. *Archiv. Secret. Vat.*, v. 227, p. 185.

86   Encyclical letter *Acerbo nimis, Acta Pii* X, II, p. 75.

87   CIC, cc. 1330-1332.

88   1 Cor 2:4.

89   Cf. *Archiv. Secret. Vat.*, v. 227, p. 18.

90   Cf. ibid.

91   Cf. *Archiv. Secret. Vat.*, v. 227, p. 1018.

92   Cf. ibid., v. 227, p. 18.

93   Cf. ibid., v. 227, p. 290.

94   Cf. ibid., v. 227, p. 999.

95   Cf. ibid., v. 227, p. 978.

96   Cf. ibid., v. 3900, p. 1554.

97   Encyclical letter *Mystici Corporis*, AAS 35 (1943) 235.

98   CIC, c. 125 §1.

99   Cf. encyclical letter *Mystici Corporis*, AAS 35 (1943) 235; encyclical letter *Mediator Dei*, AAS 39 (1947) 585; apostolic exhortation *Menti Nostrae*, AAS 42 (1950) 674.

100   Apostolic exhortation *Menti Nostrae*, AAS 42 (1950) 677.

101   Cf. epistle *La ristorazione, Acta Pii* X, 1, p. 257.

102   Cf. Mt 9:37.

103   Cf. *Archiv. Secret. Vat.*, v. 227, p. 90.

104   Cf. ibid., v. 227, p. 1021.

Thoughts By and About the Holy Curé of Ars

Power and Responsibility, Joy and Suffering for Priests in Caring for Souls

A MAN STANDING IN GOD'S PLACE

- "A priest is a man holding God's place, a man invested with all of God's powers!"
- "Look at the power of a priest! The words of a priest turn a piece of bread into God! It is even more marvelous than the creation of the world."
- "A priest is someone God places on the earth as another mediator between poor sinners and the Lord, just as he himself is the mediator between us and his Eternal Father."
- "O holy and eternal Father, let us make a trade. You are holding the soul of my friend in purgatory, and I hold the body of your Son in my hands! Now then: free my friend and I will offer your Son to you with all the merits of his Passion and Death."
- "When I hold the Lord in my hands during Mass, what can he refuse me?"
- "A priest can only be properly understood in heaven."
- "O, what an incredible thing it is to be a priest! If a priest were to fully grasp it, he would die of it."

THE SUFFERING AND JOY OF BEING A PRIEST

- "O, how frightening it is to be a priest! Confession! The sacraments! What a responsibility! If we knew what it meant to be a priest, we would flee like the saints to the desert to avoid becoming one!"
- "What fears should not grip a humble priest when exercising such a tremendous ministry [that is, absolution]?"

- "If a priest were truly penetrated by the greatness of his ministry, he would be unlikely to survive."
- "No! There is nothing in the entire world less happy than a priest. How does he spend his life? Witnessing offenses against God. A priest sees nothing other than this."
- "He is always like St. Peter at the praetorium. He always has our Lord before his eyes: insulted, scorned, and battered with insults. . . . O, if I had known what it meant to be a priest, I would have immediately saved myself by entering a Trappist monastery instead of the seminary!"
- "The priesthood is such a burdensome office that if a priest did not have the consolation and joy of celebrating the Holy Mass, he would not be able to bear it."
- "A priest must experience the same joy as the Apostles when he sees our Lord, held in his hands."

What It Means to Be a Pastor

- "Being a priest does not trouble me. Not at all! I can celebrate Mass! But I would not want to be a pastor: that troubles me."
- "I would gladly get up at midnight! It is not the hard work that frightens me; I would be the happiest of priests were it not for the thought of having to present myself before the tribunal of God as a pastor."
- "If I had known everything I would have to endure as a pastor, I would have died of fright."
- "My friend, you do not know what it means to pass from a rectory to the tribunal of God!"
- He felt his pastoral responsibility so strongly that he tried to abandon the parish on more than one occasion. He would have liked to retire to a Trappist monastery.
- From the moment he was named pastor of Ars, he felt his responsibility for the parish. He had no sense of superiority, but was well aware of his importance: he knew he had become not just the representative of God before his 230 parishioners—particularly when at the altar or the pulpit—but also the representative of those 230 souls before God. . . . And since so few of those 230 souls rendered to God the tribute of

love due to him in justice, he thought it was he himself—the head of the parish—who should substitute "that portion of the love of God" lacking in the village. . . . This conviction spontaneously led him to do the penances that his parishioners—who were dedicated to work and pleasure—did not do. He felt personally responsible for every sin committed in Ars, and thought he should offer expiation for those he represented. He multiplied his penance by 230 so that his prayer as a pastor would be truly acceptable to the Lord."

- "It has been said that you give small penances to great sinners." "Of course. The confessor has to take on a part of [the penance]."

- "A priest is not a priest for himself. He does not give absolution to himself. He does not administer the sacraments to himself. He does not exist for himself: he exists for you."

Man of God

On March 12, 1959, the centennial of the death of the Holy Curé of Ars, Pope John XXIII welcomed the priests participating in a conference organized by the Apostolic Union of Secular Priests with a papal audience, and he gave the following speech.

Amid the universal concerns of the Supreme Pontificate, it comforts us greatly to observe the solid unity and wonderful harmony that the diocesan clergy offer before our gaze. Like the flame atop a candlestick, like a city raised on a mountain, theirs is a peaceful and generous force that edifies souls by example alone and makes the sanctifying work of the Church shine with a brilliant light. Today as always, our priests uphold noble ideals. They cultivate the desire for a perfect priestly life that does not fall to compromises with the spirit of the times; they seek to strengthen the bonds of priestly brotherhood so that, having overcome the narrow limits of loneliness, each one's spiritual and pastoral life may mature with redoubled fervor and greater efficacy; and they apply themselves with indefatigable concern to analyzing and solving the ever new problems facing their modern apostolate.

We take immense pleasure in this. But on the other hand, we are not ignorant of the dangers: the *inimicus homo* never stops sowing, even amid the holiest of works. Nor does it escape us that a misplaced sense of achievement and a restless search for novelty can lead to a dangerous loss of authentic priestly virtues. We therefore wish to share a few thoughts with you about today, so that contemplation of the greatness and the duties of your shared priesthood may serve as encouragement in firmly and steadfastly preserving your commitment to make the service with which the Lord has entrusted you as perfect as possible.

1. A priest is first and above all a man of God, "*vir Dei*." This is the idea that the Christian people have of you, the basis on which they judge you, and what the Lord wishes you to be. Therefore, strive to conform your lives to the pure thoughts that this definition—in and of itself—elicits in your hearts. By saying "man of God," everything that is not "of God" is excluded for a priest. A true priest is one who has chosen like Abraham to be the "father of a host of nations" (Gn 17:4) and has forever abandoned everything else to follow the divine voice. Indeed, Abraham was told by God, "Go forth from the land of your kinsfolk and from your father's house to a land that I will show you" (Gn 12:1). For a true priest, the cross is raised on this promised land. He seeks nothing other than Christ, and "this Christ crucified." In effect, the eternal and invisible God reveals himself in Jesus, and a priest must have his eyes trained to discover the "mediator between God and the human race" (1 Tm 2:5) indicated by the Father: "Have I been with you for so long a time and you still do not know me . . . ? Whoever has seen me has seen the Father" (Jn 14:9).

Through ardent love for him, may your lives therefore be filled with the fragrance of Christ, who guides us to the Father. This is the true basis for a priestly life filled with intimate peace that irresistibly enraptures other souls. Therefore we say to you: "Love of Christ and love of silence." May Jesus Christ be your only friend and comforter, whether during vigils before the tabernacle, while studying at your desk, while caring for the poor and the sick, or in the ministry of holy preaching. Seek him alone, contemplating human things in his light so you may conquer them for him. Take his easy yoke and his light burden upon yourselves, practicing the virtues proper to a consecrated life: dedication to the Lord and to all souls, tireless work for the Church, practice of the fourteen works of mercy, ready and sincere obedience to the bishop, and total respect with virile tenderness for all things holy.

Jesus cannot be found in a dissipated life, even if the most sacrosanct justifications for the ministry are invoked. For this reason we have also talked about the "love of silence." Silence is the sure guardian of all virtues, and particularly of chastity and charity; it is a guarantee for effective pastoral work.

In all that you do, therefore, may you forever be true men of God, silently committed to the quest for perfection and charity "in Jesus Christ our Lord."

2. We wish to share with you, venerable brothers and beloved sons, another familiar thought that we already proclaimed to the faithful in Rome and throughout the world on the day we took possession of our Cathedral, the Lateran Archbasilica. Explaining the majestic meaning of the solemn liturgical rite, we drew attention to the two most precious objects of the altar: "*the Book and the Chalice.*" And we said, "The bishop and all priests working together with him express the fundamental character of the pastoral mission of the Church: the teaching of sacred doctrine. Here are the two testaments in the missal; here is the fundamental and highest point of the Catholic priesthood in proclaiming to the people. . . . It is here . . . that we wish to affirm first and foremost the sacred nature of the pastoral ministry: vigorous, radiant, and enrapturing catechesis." In repeating these words again today, we desire to point you to the Sacred Scripture as the primary source of true doctrine and as healthy nourishment for your pastoral mission. Compendiums, homiletic handbooks, and even the most thorough theological journals are insufficient if this foundation is lacking; and colorful, subtly seductive printing is all the more insufficient for your intellectual and inner life, for it disrupts a consecrated soul's intimate silence and dialogue with his God. As our Predecessor St. Gregory the Great observed, "Indeed, the heart becomes lost in speaking with men; and having established with certainty that it loses its place under the pressure of turmoil caused by external concerns, it must take constant care to rise again through dedication to sacred study."

We therefore encourage assiduous study of the Sacred Scriptures, theology, and the sacred sciences in the light of the living ecclesiastical Magisterium, that it may keep you always young in spirit and protect you from the danger of imparting incorrect, vague, presumptuous, or monotonous teachings to others. Souls are seeking the word of Christ, and priests must share it with them in its completeness and freshness.

"Here is the Chalice, alongside the Book," we continued. "The most mysterious and sacred part of the Eucharistic Liturgy revolves around the Chalice of Christ, which contains his precious Blood. Jesus is our Savior, and we mystically participate in his Body, the Holy Church. Christian life is sacrifice. In charity-inspired sacrifice we find the merit for our conformation to the final purpose of Christ's earthly life." Still today, we exhort you with fatherly affection to make the Sacred Mysteries the center of your daily lives. *There is no perfection or true love of God and Christ without profound devotion to the Eucharist, which is the life of all believers but particularly of priests.* In it, the Lord gently invites us by example to put all our energy into working for souls, to love sacrifice, and to be "obedient to death, and death on a cross" (Phil 2:8).

A priest who lives on the Book and the Chalice preserves his vocation intact "until the day of Christ Jesus" (Phil 1:6).

3. As a final thought for our conference, we recommend to you another great form of love that should transfigure your life: *love of souls.* We know very well that this is your aim, but do not think our warning unnecessary. It stems from a thought that pains all shepherds of souls: after so much effort, so many sacrifices, and endless sowing, why is the harvest often reaped so little? After all the means of the apostolate are used, why do the dead children of the Church not rise, like the child who remained lifeless despite the efforts of the prophet Elisha's servant? "The boy had not awakened" (2 Kgs 4:31).

Spiritual miracles sometimes do not occur because the intention is not always pure, perhaps because we are not always and exclusively seeking the good of these souls and sacrificing ourselves for them, or perhaps because we confide too much in human and therefore weak means, without grounding them in prayer and total sacrifice.

True love of souls must therefore mean constant and intense work toward personal holiness, making use of the classic means instilled with particular insistence by the Church especially during the period of Lent: "This kind [of evil spirit] can only come out through prayer" (Mk 9:29). This must therefore mean love of prayer, contemplation, and penitential practices: a constant search for ascetic improvement, without employing methods that excessively restrain or humiliate one's personal maturity.

In sharing these thoughts with you, a brilliant example comes before our eyes and yours in the radiant figure of the Holy Curé of Ars, who truly lived the ideals of the priestly life above and beyond all rhetoric and posing. He was a man of God: he loved the altar and the pure sources of Revelation, touched souls with the mystical shepherd's staff of purification, and actively cooperated in their salvation. It has been said that "we will never know how many graces of conversion were obtained through the prayers and especially through the Holy Masses offered by the Curé of Ars." And his simple and sure preaching descended into the hearts of all to work wonders of grace even though he had once been considered poorly endowed with intellectual gifts! What better proof that only God's power working through his docile instruments—and not human resources—is capable of winning over souls?

Thoughts By and About the Holy Curé of Ars

A Life of Prayer

TURN TO GOD

- "Man is so great that nothing on earth can satisfy him. He can only be happy when he turns to God. . . . Take a fish out of water, and it will cease to live. There you have it: the same thing happens to man without God."

- "When we are before God, hours pass by like minutes. It is like foretasting heaven."

- "I do not tell him anything. I look at him and he looks at me. How wonderful it is, my children, how wonderful!"

- "Being a friend of God, being united to God . . . living in the presence of God, living for God. What a beautiful life! What a beautiful death! . . . Everything before God's eyes, everything with God, everything for God's delight. . . . What could make life more wonderful?"

- "Man was created out of love. That is why he is so given to loving."

- "The only happiness we can have on earth is loving God and knowing that God loves us."

- "If I were sad, I would immediately go confess."

- He always prayed the breviary on his knees . . . resting his gaze every once in a while on the tabernacle, with such a soft smile that it seemed as if he truly saw our Lord.

- "Does a fish perhaps seek trees and plains? . . . No. It throws itself into the water. Does a bird perhaps remain on the ground? No, it raises itself into the air in flight. Yet man, who was created to love God and be filled with God, does not love him and turns his affections elsewhere!"

- "Compared to the saints, I am an ass. But I wish to act as they do; I wish to tell you, O Lord, what they tell you."

Like a Drop of Water in the Ocean

- "One who receives Holy Communion becomes lost in God like a drop of water in the ocean: they can no longer be separated."
- Communion was the only time when he took longer than other priests.
- "I do not like it when people immediately begin to read after having received Communion: what good are the words of men when it is God who is speaking? . . . We should imitate those folks who are very curious and stand listening outside the doors."
- "A lack of devotion to the Body and Blood of our Lord Jesus Christ is a sign of reprobation [rejection by God]."

He Chose the Church as His Home

- From the beginning of his time as pastor of Ars, his happiness came from spending long hours in the church, both day and night, before the Blessed Sacrament.
- He seemed to have chosen the church as his home.
- He recommended that his parishioners do as he did; through his steady and zealous encouragement, he gently introduced many of them to the practice of visiting the Blessed Sacrament.
- "What is the Lord doing in the tabernacle? He is waiting for us."
- "Instead of looking around when we are before the Blessed Sacrament, let us close our eyes and mouths and open our hearts, and the Lord will open his; we will go to him and he will come to us, one to ask and the other to give: it will be like exchanging a breath of air."
- "When we can no longer enter the church, let us turn toward the tabernacle. No wall can block the Lord."
- "When we are traveling and see a church bell tower, it should make our hearts leap as a bride's heart leaps at the sight of the roof under which her lover resides."
- His happiness came from seeing the church and the tabernacle well adorned.

PRAYING LIKE WE BREATHE

- "We should never interrupt God's presence, just as we never interrupt our breathing."
- "As important as our work may be, we can always pray without harming our affairs."
- When the vast numbers of pilgrims kept him from devoting himself to his lengthy prayers, he chose a meditation topic in the morning and referred everything he did during the day back to it.
- Around four o'clock in the morning, those who lived near the church could see a lamp crossing the small cemetery and disappearing toward the bell tower door: it was the Curé on his way to pray. When a poor man rang the doorbell of the rectory to beg for alms, the Curé came out of that door; in fact, he had been praying. If a parishioner entered the church for a moment, he could see a dark figure at the foot of the tabernacle in the half-light of the choir: it was the Curé in prayer. And if a peasant returning home before dawn passed close by the cemetery wall, he could see a lamp leaving the church and swinging in the hands of the Curé, who had just finished praying at that moment.

APOSTOLIC PRAYER

- It was this living faith [and this burning love for the Eucharist] that led him to desire the priesthood and to work for the glory of God and the salvation of souls.
- "Only through [contact with] God can we understand what sin really means."
- "The saints understood the gravity of the offense that sin causes to God."
- "The Lord has let us know now how much it pleases him when we pray for poor sinners."
- He was happy to pray for the souls in purgatory, but he felt most at home when praying for sinners. He did not feel at peace if he did not pray for them.
- "When I preach I often have to deal with deaf and sleeping people; but when I pray I deal with God, and God is not deaf."

- When he had to address something important or decide on a delicate issue, he prayed with even greater fervor, redoubling his mortifications and fasts.

Hundreds of Strange Thoughts

- "But why is it that when we pray our spirit becomes filled with hundreds of strange thoughts that would oftentimes never come to mind if we were not praying?"
- "We should always dedicate at least fifteen minutes to preparing ourselves well for properly understanding the Mass."
- "A prayer said without preparation is a prayer poorly said."
- "How pleasing it is to [God] when we take even a short fifteen minutes away from our other doings, from some pointless conversation, for him!"

Where the Devil Starts

- "When the devil wants to lead a person astray, he starts by making him feel a great distaste for prayer."
- "A lack of daily meditation is the reason there are so many lax, lukewarm, and indifferent people."
- "Good Christians are like birds with large wings and small feet that cannot stay on the ground for long because they would no longer be able to get back up and would be preyed upon; that is why they make their nests on cliff edges, on house roofs, or in other high places. Likewise, Christians must always stay up high: as soon as we lower our thoughts to the earth, we are quickly preyed upon."
- "If I wanted to paint you a precise picture of a lukewarm soul, I would say that it is like a turtle or a snail."
- "They [lukewarm souls] lack the quickness that brings you straight to God. They are burdened down by something heavy and wearisome that makes them tired: oftentimes it is venial sin to which they remain attached."
- "We allow the years the Lord has granted us to pass by in total indifference, never concerning ourselves with the reason God put us here on earth."

- "A lukewarm soul does not spend a single moment thinking of how to change its condition because it believes it has a good relationship with God."
- "The greatest temptation is not having temptations."
- "The temptations we should fear most, and that lead more souls to their ruin than we might imagine, are small prideful thoughts: those self-aggrandizing thoughts, those little satisfactions of the ego in everything we do and in everything that is said about us."

What Is Harmful

- "What is harmful are these daily news stories, these conversations, these politics, and these newspapers . . . after stuffing our heads with them, we go to celebrate Mass and pray the breviary."
- "What keeps us priests away from holiness is a lack of reflection. We do not return back to ourselves; we do not know what we have done. What we need is reflection, prayer, and communion with God."
- "What a disgrace for a priest not to have an inner life! . . . But calm, silence, and concentration are necessary in order to have one."
- "It is in silence that God speaks."
- Solitude was his delight.
- "We should not wait until we enter the church to prepare ourselves for Mass."
- "The reason priests have become lax is that they no longer celebrate Mass with careful attention! Oh, dear! O Lord! How pitiful the priest who carries out this act just like any other!"
- The servant of God prayed his office in the church, on his knees. He was so deep in meditation that he noticed neither the circling crowd nor the ongoing noise.

Talking About a Saint

On November 18, 1959, at Santa Maria della Pace Church in Brescia, Italy, the archbishop of Milan, Cardinal Giovanni Battista Montini (later Pope Paul VI), brought the small diocesan synod to a close and gave a speech evoking the person and works of St. John Mary Vianney, the Curé of Ars, during year of the centennial of his death. The text was transcribed from a recording and reflects his speaking style.

It is always difficult to talk about a saint and avoid simply narrating his life story, which is always relatively easy and would also be very simple in this case. John Mary Vianney's life is not marked by major episodes or earth-shattering events: it moves uniformly throughout the period that interests us, from the beginning to the end, very regularly and very simply.

If we do not wish to engage in embellished praises and instead wish to stick to reality, I believe that such a human situation is quite difficult, despite the attempts of modern hagiographers to categorize it as common. And so it happens that we feel comfortable with a saint whose life we seek to describe and whose virtues we seek to know. It almost seems as if by putting him on our own level, we too can become like him and in some sense feel that we have a right to converse with him. At a certain point, though, we realize that his stature—the stature of such a great saint—far exceeds our own by no easily quantifiable degree. Something superior, unique, exceptional, and charismatic lends the saint his privileged position and exceptionality, and we are left speechless and somewhat humiliated in recognizing that we are different from him, and perhaps even in recognizing to what extent we are different from him.

In the case of the Holy Curé of Ars, at least as far as I am concerned, the difficulty increases: it increases because there is something truly extraordinary in his very ordinary life. Certain elements come into play, such as his fascinating biographies, the popularity he has gained, and how well the writings about his life have circulated. But I think even greater difficulty arises from the fact that this saint presents himself under two aspects: our patron—for us as priests—and our model, meaning that we should be able to imitate him. Though we so readily accept him as our patron and feel comforted by such a gentle, meek, humble, attentive, and understanding person as this priest from the previous century—and to have him as our defender, to have him as our intercessor before the Lord for our needs, struggles, and aspirations—things instead become very difficult—at least for me—when it comes time to say, "I need to conform myself to him, I need to be able to imitate him."

Fortunately, this saint is one of the most heavily documented ones, as you know; I should say, there is no lack of information regarding his life. If we think of how much has been written about him, at least in France and even elsewhere, we can see that it is certainly not too hard to write about him or to come to know this admirable sight that was his life. He was one of the saints who had the honor of being canonized while still living. Many saints learn of their sainthood upon death, and many times it is almost a reinstatement carried out by public opinion and the Church herself for these saints, who are then honored alongside the altars. Just think of how many saints underwent a reexamination procedure: a reinstatement of their lives in order to be later proposed for public worship and imitation by good souls.

This saint was instead already highly renowned and very well known during his lifetime; even before his death there were short biographies and various images of him in circulation, and there were people taking care to collect his relics even before his life had ended. It has been said that something similar happened to other saints, too, such as St. Charles Borromeo. Giovanni Pietro Giussano, one of the biographers of St. Charles and his secretary during his final years, noted that by the time he wrote his biography of St. Charles—which is one of the most important ones to date—at a distance of thirty years or so from the time of his death, there were already seven other biographies in print.

Well, not even two years after the death of the Curé of Ars, two large volumes written by Alfred Monnin were already in print and are still the primary reference for his life description and facts about him. And there we see that the hope of beginning the beatification process was expressed during the funeral eulogy by the bishop of Belley, who firmly wished for the Church to recognize this exceptional person as worthy of the devotion of the Christian community.

Yet canonization and even beatification were delayed more than fifty years. But the fact is that the news of his sainthood and the acclamation of his exceptional life were immediate, and from there an extensive amount of literature emerged that had preserved his words, several homilies, various fragments, and many episodes. And so few saints received the authoritative comments that he did, and by that I mean from the popes. The popes of the past century have spoken at length about this saint to extol his virtues, illustrate his life, and recommend his example.

And so here we are after the addresses by Pius XI regarding the Holy Curé of Ars, after the many references made to him by Pius XII, and after no less than an encyclical, the most recent one, which is the source of our reflections on this saint; the encyclical was published, as you all know, by Pope John XXIII, who is felicitously reigning at present . . .

It instead seems to me that we always have some work to do in relation to this saint: not so much, I repeat, in presenting ourselves with a model we think we already know, but rather in making ourselves similar to this saint. And if we truly desire to draw closer to him, if we truly dare to bring our priestly life onto the same page as his, what should we do?

This topic is much more fitting to our simple conversation.

Priestly Awareness

And the effort, or rather the attempt, to draw closer to him immediately confronts us with a problem: examining whether our priestly awareness is similar to the Curé's awareness of his priestly life and dignity. Do we have that same idea? Do we think in the same way? We have to have a concept of ourselves. What concept of himself did the Curé of Ars have? And what is ours? Are they different? Do they coincide? Do they complement one another?

I would say that fortunately they seek one another and partly coincide. And it is one of the most beautiful things we can observe about ecclesiastical life in our time: this model has already worked in the Church of God and it has already been at least tendentiously reproduced, making it worth noting and accepting with consolation and encouragement. But from this perspective, the fact is that we need to close the distance and try as much as possible to make the Curé of Ars' consideration of himself become our own. If we start from here, we will achieve something more.

And we can identify two very obvious points in this perspective: the first, which is not unique to John Mary Vianney but I would say is common to all true saints, is an extraordinary humility.

HUMILITY

Saints are devoured by this sense of their nothingness, by this sense of disproportion between themselves and the God and Christ whom they adore and serve. This abyssal gap was first observed by the holiest of all creatures, our Lady, who in the midst of proclaiming the wonders of God—in God and in herself—in the canticle of the *Magnificat*, says that God "has looked upon his handmaid's lowliness . . . the Mighty One has done great things for me" (Lk 1:48-49).

And so it was that St. John Mary Vianney had a constant, indefatigable humility. Sometimes we are bothered by saints' statements about their own nothingness because they seem exaggerated, but we have to understand them. They are neither affectations, nor gratuitous statements, nor formalities to defend themselves against the praises people tend to give to those who prove themselves virtuous and become teachers of others. The saints truly have this sense of their own emptiness and they live it, declare it, profess it, and naturally accept the consequences if anyone disdains them for it; if anyone takes them seriously, they seem to be truly thankful. I will read a sentence or two to illustrate, as unnecessary as it is, the way St. Vianney saw himself and felt about himself.

Toward the end of his life, when another priest was assigned to help him as coadjutor, he would be heard telling his new assistant, "Oh! When you are here, some things still get accomplished. But when I am alone, oh, I am not worth a dime. I am like zeros, which have no value unless they are accompanied by another number."

And then, with a phrase that I think is just splendid from a literary perspective as well, he once exclaimed, "Oh! I still haven't lived a single day."

How many troubles he must have experienced in his life to say that not a single day so far had gone as it should have. And when someone would start directing gestures of esteem or honor toward him, he would joke about it, saying, "I really have to say that I must be a hypocrite, because I somehow manage to deceive everyone."

And in *Le Curé d'Ars: Vie de M. Jean-Baptiste-Marie Vianney* [The Curé of Ars: Life of St. John Marie Vianney] by Alfred Monnin, which I cited earlier, there is a lithographed reproduction of one of his writings on the first page, with one phrase in particular among many similar ones that seems written with great difficulty yet much vigor: "How hypocritical I am, for I am a poor sinner."

In this priest's awareness, there is a distressing but dreadfully true sense of radical poverty, radical nothingness. Those who have not felt this sensation, which has something of the metaphysical and of the psychological abyss to it, have not drawn close to the mindset of the Holy Curé of Ars.

Priestly Dignity

At the same time, together with this incredible humility, an unparalleled sense of his own dignity almost seemed to rebound out of the depths of the abyss that he was able to dig inside himself. We need to turn to the lips of this saint, as to those of many others, but here we find a certain truth in his simplicity of expression itself that persuades us, bewilders us, and moves us: it tells of his immense sense of priestly dignity.

As you know, all contemporary literature plays on these two elements: a priest's humility and his sense of dignity and authority. The priest protagonists of many novels are portrayed as humble men hiding something immeasurably magnanimous and incomparably worthy.

And this man, who feels his own destitution to be the least reparable of all, also feels that he has within himself a certain dignity, strength, and mystery that he never stops celebrating and never shrinks from admitting with the same sincerity and acknowledgment by which he proclaimed himself destitute.

Here are a few more words from the Curé of Ars: "A priest can only be properly understood in heaven," which means that even here we have something before us that surpasses our understanding. We will never comprehend ourselves enough: we ourselves became subject to mystery the day that the rains of grace poured down upon us, first in becoming Christian, then in becoming representatives and ambassadors of Christ, and finally in becoming his ministers and priests.

He continues by saying that if a priest were thoroughly infused with an understanding of the greatness of his ministry, he would be overwhelmed, would hardly survive, and would remain nearly paralyzed by it. It would impend inside of him and on top of him as an unbearable burden: "If we could understand the priesthood on earth, it would perhaps be enough to kill us, yet not by fear, but by love."

In virtue of his powers, a priest is greater than an angel: "[The priesthood is] love of the Most Sacred Heart of Jesus," and we could abundantly confirm this point with a multitude of citations.

For this reason, I think that having self-awareness is one of the first tributes we can offer if we do not wish the centennial celebration for the Curé of Ars to be completely in vain. Let us try to closely trace our awareness around these two focal points of his mindset, of his priestly awareness. And I should say that we already know from ancient philosophy— which considered knowing oneself the core of wisdom—that acquiring self-awareness is always an arduous and important task.

We who clearly have something unique, who have a clearly decisive function in the lives of others, who are in communication with the mysteries of God, and who are at the same time physicians in communication with all of the ills of humanity, must have a self-knowledge proportionate to this priestly nature and its functions.

Will we find it difficult? Yes, it is difficult. Why? Well, because, I would say, there is a danger in this very act of reflecting on ourselves: the act of reflecting might dizzy us and make our heads spin.

The priestly dignity itself that we possess can, I would say, spellbind us. If we choose to be so enraptured with it, we present ourselves to our audience—to the historical context surrounding us—as full of an ambition that others observe and that no one would expect to find in us, and perhaps it is rooted in this kind of thinking: I have been lifted so high, I am better than others, I am no longer like a layperson or one of the common people, I am distinguished from the common people, and others should acknowledge this. And there we have it: our entire priestly mindset becomes driven by an engine of ambition and pride.

Ambition?

If we then think that on top of our dignity we also have power and authority—or in other words, that we direct the fate of many other souls, have the keys to the Kingdom of Heaven, and thereby have a right in our hands—this can also create a certain thrill and alter the true priestly awareness that we have of ourselves; in other words, we might present ourselves to others as the law. Here I am, I am in charge, and there is no one above me. You must all obey me. It is an idea that has taken root even among our clergy, particularly in past years and past centuries when spiritual authority was accompanied by temporal authority and the two powers became fused: the sword and pastoral work. The idea took hold in us that it was necessary to command as much as possible in order to administer well. What I would almost call a feudal priestly mindset arose. The priest remained distant, commanded by signals, and had to be obeyed before even uttering a word; the priest closed himself in a small circle far from the people, and a good people in this perspective would be an extremely obedient flock demanding very little, not disrupting the schedule, and leaving the priest to his majestic self-contemplation and this untroubled life of his ministry. And so I repeat: there is a danger that even the effort to develop priestly self-awareness based on the truth of the mystery carried out in us by the Sacrament of Ordination might alter a genuine priestly awareness.

Instead, according to what the Curé of Ars teaches us by his twofold mindset, we need to correct our mentality and then attempt to make it as Christ wills it, because St. Vianney's mindset is no different from the one that Christ preaches: yes, our dignity is immense, yes, our authority is uncontestable, but then what does all this mean? Why are we priests?

PRIESTS TO SERVE

We are priests to serve. Our dedication is functional: may the first become last, may the first serve others. We function for others, not for ourselves, and we must firmly insist on this point if we truly wish to reproduce in ourselves Christ's plan for priests, which the Curé of Ars reproduced for us and made familiar and accessible to us.

And we will see, dear brothers, how we have been made candidates for frightful things precisely because of this sublime office. Yes, we have the office of being redeemers of the world, but *redemption is achieved through the Cross*. We must redeem others by our suffering, just as Christ who was not sin became sin for us, as St. Paul says (see 2 Cor 5:21), meaning that he took onto himself all human iniquities in order to expiate and eliminate them, which brought him to the Cross. If we are priests, meaning that if we are the heads, the guides, and the examples for others, we must take this tremendous weight of expiation for others upon our shoulders. You will see in certain writings and in certain moments of the life of the Curé of Ars how this weighed down upon his humble yet clairvoyant priestly awareness to the point of anguish. "Oh! If I had known what it meant to be a priest," he once exclaimed, "perhaps I would have feared receiving this grace from the Lord."

He felt responsibility in a way that few others do. He felt charged with expiation for the sins of others. He did penances in place of his penitents. He felt crushed by the sins of the world around him and charged with the duty of becoming the victim of this situation. Priests are at the center of this clash between good and evil, grace and sin, God and the devil. And we know full well that this clash is sacrifice: it is the Cross. This is the priestly awareness of the Holy Curé of Ars that we must strive to make our own.

PRIESTLY SPIRITUALITY

If this is the way we are approaching the Holy Curé of Ars, then a second aspect to consider arises: it is what we could call spirituality. What do we mean by "spirituality"? It is a popular word that runs off everyone's lips with the greatest of ease. I think that the definition given by a Spanish writer is correct, when he says that "it is the way in which we seek to fulfill the ideal of the Christian life and we can also say of the priesthood."

How can we practice and fulfill this aim of the priesthood? How did the Curé of Ars fulfill and practice it? In other words, we have to find the operating principles, the main ideas, and the development parameters of this awareness; we have to see whether his spirituality—the way he lived his life, the development of his outside awareness, and his manifestations in action and virtue—can be followed by us, and if so, how.

You know that in following this insight, this expression of the life of the Curé of Ars, the encyclical cites three very basic elements. We are shocked to find nothing in the encyclical that talks about the saint's singular, prodigious, and miraculous displays; we could say that they have been deliberately forgotten so there would be nothing in this saint's celebratory description that might not also console us and invite us to imitate him.

The first aspect the encyclical presents is *asceticism*: spiritual exercise, struggle, and penance. And what an asceticism it was! Then the second aspect is the ascent of the soul, *prayer*, contact with God, or conversation with this present and invisible *Alter* (Other), the Blessed Sacrament: this tension of a soul always projected beyond itself toward this transcendence that remains so close, confiding, and fatherly, but yet so mysterious, sublime, and worthy of all tribute of the very best kind our soul can offer.

And finally the third point presented by the encyclical is *pastoral zeal*: serving souls both from a formal priestly perspective as well as actually feeding or nourishing the spiritual lives of others.

EXTRAORDINARY IN THE ORDINARY

Having said these things that I believe give us a complete overview, we are led to an observation that has been repeated by those who have spoken of the Curé of Ars during this period, which is the following: he lacks originality. This says it all. Who among us does not try to humble himself and to live a disciplined and ordered life anyway? Our life itself, signed by the marvelous yoke of ecclesial celibacy, is already a penance. And who among us does not pray anyway? We take the breviary and the Missal in hand every day, and we could even say from dawn till dusk. And who is not devoted to the Eucharist, when the Eucharist is precisely the center of our life of piety and of our liturgical ceremonies? And who among us is not completely outstretched in the service of others? And everything we do is part of the ordinary routine. Here, dear brothers, is what should draw us close to the Curé of Ars: precisely this lack of peculiarity, new formulas, capricious originality, or anything that might carry us far from the main road of a priesthood devoted to the care of souls.

"The figure of the Curé of Ars," writes Msgr. Giovanni Colombo, the rector of our seminary in Milan, "is sketched out by the encyclical. It is a figure entirely carved from the living substance of the Catholic priesthood that—precisely because of its substance—is never out of fashion, never loses its force, and never grows old; in fact, it precedes all times because it belongs to all times. His figure is made up of few elements, none of which is new, but is entirely drawn forth from the most common traditions, and all its elements are derived from the pure and extreme quintessence of the priesthood: celebrating Mass and praying the breviary, preaching and confessing, meditating and doing penance, and carrying out works of mercy. The simple greatness of the pastor of Ars is all here in these actions repeated with exasperating monotony, but united with an ever more scrupulous fidelity, an ever deeper spirit of reflection and meditation, an ever more crystalline purity of heart, and an ever growing and more ardent love."

MODERN RELEVANCE OF THE MESSAGE OF ARS

Despite his encouragement of a holy search for suitable forms of pastoral care, the Holy Father's presentation of the figure of St. John Vianney in these terms suggests that we should not look too far away. When faced with the inadequacy of our priestly service, we often readily blame out-dated methods, and often rightfully so. But if priests today are in need of new methods, the pope teaches that their greatest and most urgent need is personal depth and *attention to the essentials*. And this will be a very difficult task, but without it even the most updated methods will remain ineffective.

And I repeat that this is an aspect observed by those who have stopped to examine, at least during this centennial celebration, the Curé of Ars. Lochet, a highly authoritative Belgian author, says, "The extraordinary modern relevance of the message of the Holy Curé of Ars comes from the fact that he does not introduce a unique form of action or a new method of apostolate fitting to his time and therefore quickly left behind. In fact, he does not proclaim a truth linked to time, but an eternal message: a message that transcends the accidental characteristics of an era, an ever-relevant message. Indeed, what strikes us when we reflect on the whole life of the Holy Curé of Ars is the fact that the progressive development of his life was not made up of a series of movements or advancements, but a spiritual focus on and deepening exploration of a single role: pastor."

HOLINESS

And so here arises a common and recurrent question that is always worth reflecting on: it is the possibility that we so-called secular or diocesan priests—however we wish to say it, perhaps with the correction that Cardinal Mercier suggested, we priests who are launched into the ordinariness of priestly life—have of becoming holy and perfect.

And we are certainly left in a state of perplexity. Why? Because we are missing some of the excellent means that make Christian perfection easier and more accessible: we are missing religious vows as well as all of the provisions and lifestyle organization that the religious life seeks to provide to make us better equipped and lead us down a quicker and more efficacious path to achieving holiness.

And so, even in talking about our own conditions, we must look with admiration and even a bit of envy to our religious brothers, who have instead courageously chosen and obtained from Divine Providence the vocation of putting themselves on an organized path to holiness, in the conditions to attain perfection. But are we then second-class priests? Are we poor wretches? Should we be happy with occupying a secondary place in God's paradise? Or is there instead some possibility of recovery, some way of becoming holy without this sublime organization of our lives in search of holiness? We must sacrifice certain means, which are excellent and of the highest degree. So are we left unsupplied? No, we are not. We can find the source of holiness in the object of our priesthood: the charity in which our priesthood is steeped.

The pastoral priesthood is the one that directly receives the defending charity of God, in its essence and in the greatest amount. It is the one that most fulfills God's desire to infuse all people with love, and it sits right along the line intersecting this divine intention. The Lord wants to save the world and has chosen someone. That someone is us. This charity passes directly to the form of priesthood destined to take that charity and pour it out in turn on others. There is no greater charity than to give one's life for others, and these are Christ's words (see Jn 15:13). We are not on the systematic path to holiness, but we are on the line taken by Christ and taught to us by Christ in order to become holy: Christ's holiness. We can find the inexhaustible source of holiness in our own lifestyle, just as it is, just as described and regulated by canon law. And take note: we have to find it. Woe to us if we believe that because we do not have the perfecting commitments of religious vows we can say, "We can be less perfect, less observant, and less loving. We can take it slow while others run and fly. We can just move forward while taking it easy."

More is expected of us because we have a greater inheritance of charity to administer, receive, and give; more is expected of us because we are responsible for more; more is expected of us because we have more contact with the liturgy, which celebrates the mysteries of grace by the sacraments; more is expected of us because we are in continual communication with other souls.

We are actively involved, and this was even said by St. Thomas Aquinas, the very Doctor of the Church who praised and defended the greatness and the dignity of religious vows and the religious state: the commitment to holiness required of priests serving souls is greater than that of religious priests. For a religious priest, holiness is something acquired or in the process of being acquired; we are instead obliged to practice holiness, and this is something that even stirs us, causes us to tremble, and almost makes us—like the Curé of Ars—want to flee.

We must master these things, and we must make them immanent in our priesthood: *holiness and charity*. We are in the exercise of holiness, *in exercenda perfectione*, and not *in acquirenda perfectione* like those in the religious state. And we are less sustained by means that provide order, remove dangers, make virtues easier, sustain good examples, and regulate comforts. If we desire to meet the demands of our vocation, it is much more necessary for us to galvanize in ourselves this sense of closeness to Christ, imitation of him, reception of every grace from him, life according to him, and self-sacrifice like his.

TEMPTATIONS TO ESCAPE

This means precisely that we should have an inner adherence to our profession as priests caring for souls. Note that we priests often develop an attitude I would consider evasive, grumbling, and presumptuous in thinking that if we were somewhere else things would be better, and that we are misunderstood, undervalued, not yet promoted, or not appreciated for what we have done and can do; and we try to console ourselves with these imaginings about the natural and human satisfactions missing in our ministry.

This is self-deception, dear sons and brothers, and this is not the mindset of the Curé of Ars. The Curé of Ars teaches us that we need to take responsibility for our mission, whatever it is, and I would say to be pleased with it, giving it our all and never seeking to avoid it. The Curé of Ars felt the burden of his priesthood so strongly, we were saying earlier, that he too had his moments with the temptation to escape and flee because he could no longer handle it. He was called back, and we all know how, and he himself confessed that this was the truth and this was the life. And the very day he was made canon—with all due respect to other canons—he immediately sold the mozzetta he was given for the occasion.

And when they wanted to offer him a more important parish than the one where he was working with less than three hundred souls, he refused: "This is enough for me, this is enough for me and I must remain here." And for forty years, his entire pastoral life remained centered on that same small area, on that same clump of earth he had been charged with cultivating.

He showed an inner and outer adherence to his ministry and to his office here with an obedience I believe equivalent to that of any priest giving obedience to his superior in the religious life. Our *promitto* at times involves demands that are neither easy nor light, and offering ourselves with loyalty and perseverance to this initial promise can truly be a wellspring that perfects our lives, but more than anything it becomes a source that renders our lives tremendously and fruitfully holy.

Msgr. Guerry, who studied the spirituality of the diocesan clergy years ago, also observed the same thing. He said, "The uniqueness of the diocesan clergy is rightly that of having an unspecified spiritual approach, and therefore of being naturally closer than anyone else to the general spirituality of the Church. Because of the duties of his state, a priest of the parish clergy has to become everything for everyone, available to all the souls in his care whatever their peculiarities. He is at the service of the Christian people, and for this reason—given the general nature of this type of clergyman—we can find a closer relationship with the liturgy in him than in others, particularly with the liturgy of the Sacrament of the Eucharist. He is at the service of that liturgy, which should give life to the Christian people."

This is the spirituality of the Curé of Ars, and this is how similar it is to what we are daily presented with in our routine and customary lifestyle.

Efficacious Means

And here a final point for consideration arises: if this is the plan and this is the way of living our priesthood, what are the means? The means? The way we put it into practice? How do we fit it to our real circumstances? How do we apply it to the current circumstances that surround us? This adherence to our ministry, and the need to make it efficacious and extend it to a greater number of believers, brings us down to earth and harasses us with many questions.

I think that every honest priest must be at least somewhat tormented by this question: "So do I have efficacious means in my hands or not? Do these systems with which the Church has provided me work, or have they become old and run down? How was this canon law developed? On the basis of what historical reasons? On the basis of what relation to public and private law? And it is still here, immovable! Let's hope a council will come and change it a bit! Everyone is expecting this reform to update the Church of God. And this blessed Latin! Oh dear, I have to preach to the people and I am talking to them in a language they do not understand." There is a rightful impatience that is a measure of zeal, and it leads us directly to this practical application of the duties of our priesthood.

And yet, if I may, based on the little experience I have been gaining from direct pastoral visitations, I would call on you to be attentive to three temptations that may arise from this search for means.

The first temptation is to limit our ministry to the search for means. You might say the following: "I am going to build a small chapel, I have to build the church, I have to pay the debts, I need to publish a book, and I have to set up a school." These are all means.

However, if I limit my priestly activities to the search for and attainment of means, and make this the measure of my success—oh! what a good priest: he built a house, there was no rectory and he built one, there was no soccer field and he was able to make one, he put a movie projector in his parish, and so forth, which I repeat are all means that we should certainly be concerned with—and if my plan for priestly accomplishment remains only this, then I am a priest who has understood neither our time, nor the example of the Curé of Ars, nor the mystery of Christ working through me. And how many of us stop there, and how painful it is to see that so many religious realities never reach the people unless accompanied by sign-up sheets or letters asking for more means. Just a few days ago, a good workman—the grammatical errors and handwriting of his letter made his trade clear—wrote me saying, "Goodness! Every morning I find requests for contributions, enrollments, subscriptions, and offers in my mailbox: all for things I have never even seen before. I have no idea how they got my address."

UTILITARIANISM

And in these simple souls, these souls already shaken by the attacks of faithlessness and perhaps already wounded by atheistic objections, the religious world comes to be perceived in this way: a constant search coming from unknown sources hounding these people with persistent requests for money for works they will never even have the chance to see or to experience and that they should associate—with great difficulty—with a world dedicated to God. This is not good publicity, and it is not good priesthood.

There is also another tendency in our religious practices of turning piety into something utilitarian. This is a saint that brings in lots of offerings, who has an image with candles: he will make a good source of income. If we give the church this name, if we build it immediately, and so forth, it will give us a better profit.

This is not the religion God intended; this is not the religion Christ intended! The reason, dear brothers, and let us be perfectly honest here, is that when the search for means for the sake of the Kingdom of God becomes so systematic and consuming, it can become a search for means for their own sake. We inadvertently—almost because of a professional bias—substitute our own person and our own interests for the interest of the cause we serve. *We often become speculators*, prospectors, and hoarders of wealth; many times we have transformed charity into forms of profit. But what will become of it the day a people, a history, and a Church will judge us, the day when God will judge us? This was my charity: it was all a gift, and you turned it into a source of speculation. When this money management should have been very scrupulous and cautious in our hands, it instead became quite self-assured and associated with all sorts of liberties and many times even with all the possible forms of injustice in this area.

Let us be rigorous in this, and the poverty of the Curé of Ars and the recommendations of the Church on this point help us feel the need we have to become freed again from the very means we wish to use to give glory to God and save souls.

"Give everything," the Curé of Ars said, "give everything and keep nothing," and practice the word of Christ as stated by St. Paul: "He became poor although he was rich" (2 Cor 8:9). Woe to anyone who would change this course set by Christ: *he was poor and became rich through being a priest.*

Reform and Staying Up-to-Date

A second danger. The following can be a second danger in this search for means: the need to find new ones, the need to reform the Church, and the need to head down roads not traveled. We must immediately clarify that staying up-to-date and using effective means are certainly not only honest but also dutiful activities. But the mentality developing nowadays is that we cannot trust in what the Church is today, in her structure, in her rule, in her authority, or in her traditional aspects, almost as though she were paralyzed by her very structure and experience, halting because of a brake that holds her back and immobilizes her rather than creating energy for action.

Let us remember that Church reform is a question of authority, and the fact that those in authority are aware of this point is certainly evident in countless ways, which sometimes even disturb us in our laziness. How many criticisms have I heard, for example, of the new translation of the Psalter approved by Pope Pius XII? But we were perfectly content with the old one! Why did he change it? And so forth and so on. But the pope has foresight: he sees that the modern world's need for understanding is such that the words should be adapted as best as possible to fulfill to it, and so forth. This appearance of the desire for reform—which I repeat is not up to us to promote, but we have to pray that the Church will bring it to us and that the Lord will enlighten his Church and guide her in accordance with his Spirit—could instill first of all a spirit of caprice, a sort of "let's give it a shot" with random attempts, and second of all—and more commonly—a spirit of criticism and dissatisfaction. Be warned that this is a form of spiritual corrosion that erodes a very precious spiritual communion particularly with our less cultured, less educated brethren.

Woe to us if our critical spirit prevents us from conversing with others, bearing with them, helping them, learning from their example, and accepting their admonitions! The spirit of criticism first begins to corrode things, and then it moves on to corrode the principle of authority and splits even our external communion with the rest of the Church. . . .

The reform, the true reform we need to pursue, is the reform of the Curé of Ars: in other words, as we said before, we need to dig deeper. If we become good, we become faithful, we become perfect, and we become saints, you will see that the Church herself will quickly be reformed.

NATURAL CAUSES

And the *third temptation* connected to the search for means, which is a point that has been extensively and widely discussed, is an exaggerated faith in natural causes: preferring natural and temporal causality to the supernatural causality of the activities affecting our inner life and the spiritual means of sanctifying and governing souls, and believing that social and political influence and the support of important people can be worth more than the influence of the saints and the humility of our destitution, moving forward as best we can.

The improper value given to temporal means, particularly with respect to the value of supernatural means, leads us off the path: it becomes an excessive search, a search that can truly make us lose our balance in our priestly activities. Yet at the same time, we reaffirm and once again invoke the authority of the Curé of Ars himself in stating that the use of helpful and evident means for our ministry—and keeping them up-to-date—is not only acceptable, but also wise and even dutiful.

The Curé of Ars started several schools, the Curé of Ars had a sense for missions, the Curé of Ars ran an orphanage, the Curé of Ars never stopped restoring his church, making chapels, and even restoring the town bell tower for—just think!—a mere three hundred souls. So he had a certain reserve that limited and prevented any exaggerated scale of action, but yet he never spoke a harsh word against so-called novel ideas or attempts to bring the people closer, choosing the approaches he found in line with their interests and aspirations in order to draw them closer.

We will immediately find the bridge if we look for those threads of the interests and aspirations of the people, even using our own tradition as a bridgehead to draw them closer, enter into dialogue, and—God willing—convert them.

Supernatural Means

But above all, dear brothers in the priesthood, and here the Holy Curé of Ars teaches us best, we need to have an immense and audacious faith in supernatural means. We have them in our hands, but do we truly believe it? Are we truly convinced that prayer can change the things of the world and the things of the soul? And if we are, do we actually turn to these living, powerful, and persistent supplications so that our ministry may become truly efficacious? Is our ministry sustained by this core of spirituality and inner dialogue with the Holy Spirit so that it may become truly efficacious?

Prayer and Penance

And along with prayer comes penance. How much penance the Holy Curé of Ars did! Certainly not all of us are called to imitate him—indeed I would say none of us is—in what we see as extreme and mysterious. Yet this self-mortification that permeated this entire life, which almost seems to sadden and impoverish it, made it so noble, dignified, and strong! We can see this phenomenon now in Padre Pio: do you think people come to see miracles? Or is it rather this aura of spirituality, and specifically of poverty and self-mortification, together with the never before seen stigmata on his hands that attract even the most distant people. These are powerful curiosities that can truly reawaken a soul's fascination. A self-mortifying priest is convincing, a priest doing penance is convincing, but a priest living the easy life—though he may preach the Gospel—is not convincing.

Catechism and Confession

Next we have the *catechism*, and then the wondrous wellspring of revival for souls that we call *confession*. Here, too, if we only knew what this sacrament is, even just humanly speaking, how modern it is, and how it has been stolen from us by all of these psychoanalysts, novelists, and other people preaching a sort of spiritualism bereft of God. What a treasure we have in our hands! And how amazing that the miraculous divine action of divine forgiveness in this sacrament can be accompanied by the human action—my action, if I exercise it—of spiritual instruction through words: the ability to factor into the fates of others, examining their souls.

What a magnificent ministry! And here as well, if we practice it even in simple forms, always discreetly but ever more attentively, profoundly, and efficaciously, we will surely never be able to find a comparable instrument.

Our efficacy depends on our ability to make use of these supernatural means in our hands: it depends on our priestly gifts, on the grace we have been endowed with, on the prayers we are always free to offer, on penance, on self-mortification, and on the poverty of life to which we are called.

And then you will see, dear brothers in the priesthood, what is to come. And here again the life of the Curé of Ars provides us with images that speak volumes, and they speak so loudly that they take our voice away and leave us silent. In other words, a man who lives his priesthood in this manner will enter into an experience of Christ himself not just in terms of an external imitation, but in terms of a certain shared life in the present moment, a self-aware reproduction of Christ in his own person.

THE SUFFERING OF THE WORLD

And we know what it was like for the Curé of Ars. He began to feel his dedication: we could say it was a painful experience for the Curé of Ars. It neither upset his calmness, nor stole his smile, nor made his daily conversation irritable or impatient, but rather made him gentle, humble, and understanding. But what inner upheaval! He lost his peace: it was sold to all the postulants and penitents who came running to him. He lost his calm view of the world, which is so lovely to us: oh, how peaceful the world is!

The Curé of Ars had a grim view of it, but why? Because he felt responsible, he felt that there was a link between himself and the world that could no longer be broken, and that he would be called to account for it one day.

That responsibility grew immeasurably as he saw how the world is full of evil. The Curé of Ars had an awareness and perception of evil that few other saints did: he had the affliction of perceiving sin for what it is.

His life can be well compared to Gethsemane. And at a certain point, as you know, this oppressive vision of the evil in the world came alive and became an apparition of the spirit of evil that tormented him, derided him, confused him, humiliated him, and tormented him, and that he fought with humility, prayer, and penance, until finally he struggled with the greatest trial that can possibly face those of us who have faith, hope, and charity: "My temptation," said the Curé of Ars, "is the despair of losing what I hold most dear!" This was his most profound and intense affliction: "I could wish that I myself were . . . separated from Christ for the sake of my brothers" (Rom 9:3). Even St. Paul brushed with and suffered this subtle, piercing, and poisonous experience of losing every good, even hope itself. The Curé did not lose it, but he felt its horrible absence, he felt it tearing away, he felt its weight, and he died with that feeling.

But outside, the small town of Ars had become Christian.

Thoughts By and About the Holy Curé of Ars

Pastoral Charity

The Good Shepherd Gives His Life for His Sheep

- "If a priest should die from working and toiling for the glory of God and the salvation of souls, it would not be a bad thing."
- "If I already had one foot through the gates of heaven and were told to go back to earth to work for the conversion of a sinner, I would gladly return. And if I were to stay there until the end of the world, getting up at midnight every night and suffering as much as I am now, I would gladly stay."
- "When it is time to talk about God, I am never tired."
- "I only rest twice a day: at the altar and at the pulpit."
- "St. Alphonsus Liguori took a vow to always remain active. We [pastors] have no need to take that vow."

Tenderness and Suffering for Unhappy Children

- "Poor sinners! If I just think that there are people in the world who will die without ever having tasted for a single moment the happiness of loving God. . . . No, sinners are truly too unhappy! . . . Too unhappy!"
- The idea that there are some people who die without experiencing the joy of loving God caused him great suffering.
- "Poor sinners, you are not happy in this life and you never will be!"
- He seemed to have a particular preference for poor sinners: he was not harsh with them.
- "How can I be harsh with people who come from so far away, make so many sacrifices, and are often forced to come here in secret?"
- "We need to be compassionate and not bitter with sinners."
- He devoted all of his energies to instilling a sense of trust in them.
- "Oh, if only I could confess in their stead!"

- "If only they would come! I would do their penances for them."
- "For my part, here is my prescription: I give them a small penance, and I do the rest myself."
- On major solemnities, and particularly at Easter, he refused to eat the usual meal in order to obtain the conversion of sinners.
- During his first months of parish life, he devoted much time to his ministry in the confessional and his ministry to the sick and often neglected to eat.

WHO SHOULD BE GIVEN PREFERENCE

- "If we have the opportunity to choose between two good works, one to help a person who loves us and one to help a person who has hurt us, precedence must be given to the latter."
- An irritating person came to find him several times a day. He received him every time with the same amiability.
- "I have never become angered with my parishioners, and I do not believe I have ever reproached them."
- His smile rarely left his lips.
- He only ever responded with kindness, even though at times his body trembled as if he had a fever.
- The least religious people in the town were those who said the most positive things about him.

CHARITY IS NOT WEAKNESS

- "Do not try to please everyone. Do not try to please someone. Try to please God."
- "You have prayed, you have become sorrowful, and you have cried. But have you fasted? . . . Have you slept on a hard floor? . . . Until you have done these things, do not think you have done everything you can."

Prayer for Priests

From August 22 to August 25, 1968, Pope Paul VI was in Colombia on his sixth international trip for the occasion of the thirty-ninth International Eucharistic Congress. On August 22, in Bogotá, he celebrated a Holy Mass in which the Sacrament of Holy Orders was conferred on 41 diaconate candidates and 161 priesthood candidates. The homily, which was an intense prayer for priests, is presented here below.

CONFORMED TO CHRIST

Lord Jesus! We give you thanks for the mystery you have accomplished through the ministry of our hands and our words, by the power of the Holy Spirit.

You have deigned to impress a new, inner, and indelible mark upon the personal being of these your chosen ones: a mark that assimilates them to you and by which each of them is and shall be called an *"alter Christus,"* an "other Christ." You have impressed your human and divine countenance upon each of them, conferring on them not only an indescribable resemblance to you, but also a certain authority, virtue, and capacity for action affirmed by the divine efficacy of your word alone and fulfilled by the divine efficacy of your will.

These your sons are yours, O Lord, and by their new title they have become your brothers and ministers. Through their priestly service, your presence and sacramental sacrifice, your Gospel, your grace, and your Spirit—in a word, the work of your salvation—will be shared with those willing to receive it; an incalculable outpouring of your charity will spread through the time of present and future generations.

These new servants of your supernatural design of love are yours, O Lord; and they are ours as well, for they are linked with us in the great work of evangelization as the most qualified collaborators in our same ministry, as our dearest children as well as brothers in our dignity and function, as valorous and unified workers for the edification of your Church, as servants and guides, as comforters and friends of the People of God, and as bestowers—like us—of your mysteries.

We give you thanks, O Lord, for this event rooted in your infinite, personal, and uniting love, and it makes us not just worthy but rather obliged to celebrate your mysterious mercy. It makes us all ready and almost impatient to run into the midst of the people, toward whom our entire life is directed, with no possibility of recovery, no limits to our self-giving, and no hidden worldly interests.

Lord, in this solemn and decisive moment, we dare to voice an ingenuous though not foolish prayer to you: O Lord, make us able to understand.

MEDIATORS BETWEEN GOD AND MAN

Lord Jesus, we are able to understand by recalling that you are the mediator between God and humanity: not a wall, but an intermediary; not an obstacle, but a path; not a wise man among many, but the one Teacher; not any prophet, but the sole necessary Interpreter of the religious mystery, the only One who unites God to man and man to God. "No one knows . . . who the Father is except the Son," you said, "and anyone to whom the Son"—which is you, O Christ, the Son of the Living God—"wishes to reveal him" (Lk 10:22). You are the authentic Revealer, you are the bridge between the kingdom of earth and the Kingdom of Heaven. Without you, we can do nothing.

You are necessary and you are sufficient for our salvation. O Lord, make us able to understand this essential truth. And make us able to understand how we—yes, we: worthless human clay taken up by your miraculous hands—have become ministers of this, your one fully efficacious mediation. It will be up to us as your representatives, as bestowers of your divine mysteries, to distribute the treasures of your word, your grace, and your example among all people, to whom our entire lives are forever dedicated as of today.

This ministerial mediation places us—fragile and humble men though we remain—in a position of dignity and honor, it is true, and of authority and exemplariness that qualifies our lives both morally and socially and tends to conform the core of our personal awareness to the one that filled your divine heart, O Christ. We, too, have been made—almost together with you, living in you—both priests and victims reaching out with all our being in order to fulfill the will of the Father with you, O Lord, obedient to the point of death as you were to the point of death on the Cross, for the salvation of the world.

But now, O Lord, what we desire to understand even better is the psychological effect that the representative nature of our mission should produce in us—the dual polarization of our mentality, our spirituality, and our activity toward these two ends that find their point of contact and simultaneity in us: God and man, in a magnificent living analogy to you, God and man.

In us, God has his living instrument, his minister, and therefore his interpreter, the echo of his voice, his tabernacle, the historical and social sign of his presence among humanity, and the burning hearth radiating his love for all people. This prodigious fact—O Lord, never let us forget it!—involves a duty that is the first and sweetest of our priestly life: intimacy with Christ in the Holy Spirit, and therefore with you, O Father; that is, the duty of an authentic and personal inner life, not just jealously protected in a full state of grace, but just as voluntarily expressed in a continual reflective act of awareness, dialogue, and loving and contemplative deliberation. The words spoken and repeated by Christ at the Last Supper, "Remain in my love" (Jn 15:9), are for us, dearest sons and brothers. In this long-desired union with Christ and Divine Revelation, which was opened to the world by him, divine and human, we find the first characteristic attitude of the minister made representative of Christ and sent by the charism of Holy Orders to existentially personify Christ in himself. This is very important for us: it is indispensible. And do not think that this absorption of our conscious spirituality in intimate dialogue with Christ stops or slows the activity of our ministry; in other words, do not think that it delays the external expression of our apostolate or perhaps leads to avoiding the bothersome and burdensome effort of dedicating our services to others and ourselves to the mission with which we have been entrusted. No, it is instead the stimulus for ministerial action and the wellspring of apostolic energy; it makes efficacious the mysterious relationship between love of Christ and pastoral dedication.

Representatives of God Among the People

In fact, this is the way our priestly spirituality as God's representatives among the people turns toward its other pole: representatives of the people before God. And this, note carefully, is not just to lavish all our work and our very hearts upon the people for love of Christ, but also—in a foregoing psychological step—to take their representation upon ourselves: we receive the People of God into our love and responsibility, and indeed into our very selves. We are not just ministers of God but also ministers of the Church; in fact, we should always recall that a priest celebrating the Holy Mass acts in the place of the people; and then in terms of the sacramental validity of the sacrifice, the priest acts "*in persona Christi*"; but in terms of its application, he acts as a minister of the Church.

And so now let us ask the Lord to instill in us a sense for the people we represent, whom we bring together in our priestly office and in our hearts, which have been consecrated for their salvation: the People of God, whom we bring together in an ecclesial community, whom we call together around the altar, and whose needs, prayers, sufferings, hopes, weaknesses, and virtues we communicate. In the exercise of our ministry of worship, we are the People of God. We unite the various conditions that make up the Christian community in our representative and ministerial office: children, young men and women, families, workers, the poor, the sick, and even the absent and inimical. We are the unifying love of the people of this world. We are their heart. We are their worshiping and prayerful voice, exulting and weeping. We are their expiation. We are the messengers of their hope!

O Lord, make us able to understand. We must learn to love the people in this way, and then serve them in this way. It will cost us nothing to serve them; rather, it will be our honor and aspiration. We will never feel socially detached from them because of the fact that we are and must be distinguished from them by our office. We will never refuse to be their brothers, friends, consolers, educators, and servants. *We will be rich with their poverty, and we will be poor amid their riches.* We will be able to understand their apprehensions and transform them not into anger and violence, but into the powerful and peaceful energy of constructive works. It will be important to us that our service be silent and selfless; sincere in constancy, love, and sacrifice; and confident that your virtue will make the day efficacious. We will always keep before us and within our spirit your One, Holy, Catholic, and Apostolic Church, traveling in pilgrimage toward her eternal destination, and we will carry our apostolic motto impressed upon our minds and hearts: "We serve as ambassadors of Christ."

ALL FAITHFUL MINISTERS OF THE LORD FOREVER

Here, Lord: these new priests and deacons will accept the uniform and duties of being your ambassadors, heralds, and ministers on this blessed earth. You, O Lord, have called them; you have now filled them with the grace, charism, and authority of priestly ordination for some, and diaconal ordination for others. May you help them all remain your faithful ministers forever.

Lord, we pray to you: that the Catholic faith may be preserved through their ministry and example; that she may be filled with new light; that she may shine through generous and active charity; that their witness may echo their bishops' witness and aid their fellow brothers' witness; that they may know how to nourish a true Christian life in the People of God; that they may have the clarity and courage of the Spirit in order to promote social justice, to love and defend the poor, and to serve those in need in our modern society with the strength of gospel love and the wisdom of the Church, our mother and teacher; and that they may always seek and find the fullness of spiritual life and the fruitfulness of their pastoral ministry in the eucharistic mystery. We pray to the Lord: Lord, hear our prayer!

Thoughts By and About the Holy Curé of Ars

Perfect Continence

If We Only Realized

- "Belonging to God, being entirely God's with no separation, the body of God, the soul of God, a chaste body, and pure soul: there is nothing more beautiful!"
- "Happy the soul that can say to God, 'O Lord, I have always belonged to you.'"
- "God so fills the pure soul with himself that it loses itself in him."
- "A pure soul shines before God like a pearl in the sun. . . . A pure soul is like a beautiful rose: the three divine Persons stoop down alongside it to breathe in its scent. It is like a crystal clear mirror reflecting the sky. The image of God is reflected in it like the sun on the water."
- "We are all like small mirrors in which God beholds himself. How do you think God can recognize himself in an impure soul?"
- "A pure soul is like a beautiful pearl. So long as it is hidden in a shell at the bottom of the sea, no one would ever be drawn to admire it; but if it is exposed to the rays of the sun, it shines and draws attention. This is what happens with pure souls: though now they are hidden to the eyes of the world, they will one day shine before the angels in the light of the sun of eternity."
- "There is nothing more beautiful than a pure soul. If we only realized this, we would never lose our purity!"
- "The good scent and good flavor of fruits are sensed to the extent that the body is healthy. In the same way, the soul perceives and penetrates the wonders of God to the extent that it is pure. Oh, if we are not pure we will never taste God!"
- "God cannot resist the prayers of a pure soul. A soul unstained by this sin will obtain everything it desires from God."

Temptations and Ways of Resisting Them

- "The most common temptations are pride and impurity. One of the best ways of resisting them is a life of activity for the glory of God. Many people abandon themselves to a lax and idle life. No wonder the devil is able to put them beneath his feet."
- "Purity comes from heaven: we have to ask it of God. If we ask for it, we will receive it. We must be careful not to lose it."
- "The more our bodies have been mortified, the more they will shine like diamonds."
- "If I experienced carnal desires, I would make use of discipline."
- "If we wish to preserve purity in soul and body, we must mortify our imagination."
- "No one showed me to what extent the soul can be freed from the senses like he did."

Never Despair

- "We should not think there is any place on earth where we can escape this struggle."
- "The greatest saints are those who were tempted most."
- "The devil tempts beautiful souls the most of all."
- "The devil does everything possible to lead us to despair."
- "When we are overwrought with temptations, we cannot allow ourselves to become discouraged."
- "When you are tempted, offer God the merit of that temptation to receive its opposing virtue."
- "How difficult it is to completely purify ourselves of this sin!"
- "Yet in this war, we can be always and everywhere victorious."

A Tangible Model
of Priestly Life:
The Holy Curé of Ars

Pope John Paul II does not merely present a reflection on the Catholic priesthood in his letter to all the priests of the Church on the occasion of Holy Thursday in 1986, but for the first time he provides a model for living: a solid and eminent example of priestly witness.

In this letter, after briefly recalling the meaning of Holy Thursday for priests ("it is the feast day of priests. It is the birthday of our priesthood, which is a participation in the one priesthood of Christ the Mediator"), the Pope takes the occasion of the bicentennial of the birthday of the Holy Curé of Ars (1786-1859) to offer this "extraordinary model of priestly life and service," because "now more than ever we are in need of his witness and intercession to confront the situations of our time in which ... evangelization is combated by growing secularization [and] ... many people are losing sight of the Kingdom of God."

We are therefore dealing with the launch of a major gospel challenge to our society and our time through the example of the Curé of Ars.

Dear Brothers in the Priesthood of Christ!

Holy Thursday, the Feast Day of Priests
1. We are once again drawing near to Holy Thursday, the day in which Jesus Christ instituted both the Eucharist and our ministerial priesthood at the same time. Christ "loved his own in the world and he loved them to the end" (Jn 13:1). As the Good Shepherd that he was, he was about to give his life for his sheep (see Jn 10:11) in order to save them, reconcile

them with the Father, and bring them to new life. And already he was offering the Apostles his Body as food, given up for them, and his Blood as drink, shed for them.

Every year, this is a great day for all Christians. Following the example of the first disciples, they come to receive the Body and Blood of Christ in the evening liturgy that renews the Last Supper. They receive from the Savior the testimony of brotherly love that is destined to guide their entire lives, and they begin to keep vigil with him in order to join themselves to his Passion. You yourselves will convoke them and guide their prayer. But this day is particularly great for us, dear brother priests. It is the feast day of priests. It is the birthday of our priesthood, which is a participation in the one priesthood of Christ the Mediator. On this day, priests throughout the entire world are invited to concelebrate the Eucharist with their bishops and to renew alongside them the promises of their priestly commitments to serving Christ and his Church.

On this occasion I draw particularly close to each of you. And as I do every year, as a sign of our priestly unity in the same priesthood, driven by the affectionate esteem I hold for you and by my duty to confirm all of my brothers in their service to the Lord, I send you this letter to help you give new life to the unprecedented gift that was conferred upon you by the imposition of hands (see 2 Tm 1:6). This ministerial priesthood, which is our portion, is also our vocation and our grace. It signs our entire life with the seal of the most necessary and demanding service there is: the salvation of souls. We are nonetheless guided by a multitude of predecessors.

The Unparalleled Example of the Curé of Ars

2. One of these predecessors remains firmly present in the Church's memory and will be commemorated in a particular way this year on the occasion of the second centennial of his birth: *St. John Mary Vianney, the Curé of Ars.*

May we all thank Christ, the Prince of Pastors, for the extraordinary model of priestly life and service that the Holy Curé offers to the entire Church and most of all to us priests.

How many of us have prepared for the priesthood or carry out our difficult work as shepherds while keeping the paragon of St. John Mary Vianney before our eyes! His example cannot fall into oblivion. Now more than ever we are in need of his witness and intercession to confront the situations of our time in which, despite the presence of certain signs of hope, evangelization is combated by a growing secularization that neglects contemplation of the supernatural, many people are losing sight of the Kingdom of God, and even in pastoral work there is often too much concern for exclusively social issues and temporal objectives. In the past century, the Curé of Ars had to confront difficulties that may have presented themselves differently but were no less immense. Through his life and work he represented a major gospel challenge for the society of his time, bearing wonderful fruits of conversion. There is no doubt that he still presents us today with this *major gospel challenge*.

I therefore invite you to reflect upon our priesthood in light of this extraordinary pastor who showed us the complete fulfillment of the priestly ministry together with the holiness of the minister.

You know that John Mary Baptist Vianney died in Ars on August 4, 1859, after about forty years of exhausting dedication. He was seventy-three years old. When he first arrived, Ars was an obscure village in the Diocese of Lyons and is today in the Diocese of Belley. Toward the end of his life people were flocking there from all over France, and upon his death the fame of his holiness immediately drew the attention of the universal Church. St. Pius X beatified him in 1905; Pius XII canonized him in 1925 and then in 1929 declared him the patron of pastors throughout the world. On the centennial of the saint's death, Pope John XXIII wrote the encyclical letter *Sacerdotii Nostri Primordia* to present the Curé of Ars as a model of priestly life and asceticism, of piety and eucharistic worship, and of pastoral zeal in the context of the needs of our time. Here I would just like to draw your attention to some fundamental points that can help us to rediscover and better live out our priesthood.

THE TRULY EXTRAORDINARY LIFE OF THE CURÉ OF ARS

His Tenacious Will to Prepare Himself for the Priesthood

3. The Curé of Ars is above all a model of willpower for those preparing themselves for the priesthood. The continuous succession of many trials could have discouraged him: the effects of the revolutionary storm; the lack of formal instruction in his rural home; his father's reluctance; the need to help with the work in the fields; the risks of military service; and above all, despite his intuitive intelligence and good sensitivity, his

great difficulty with learning and memorizing and therefore with taking theology and Latin classes, ultimately leading to his dismissal from the seminary in Lyons. However, since the authenticity of his vocation had been recognized, he was allowed to be ordained a priest at age twenty-nine. With tenacity in work and prayer, he overcame all obstacles and limitations then as he would later, when during his priestly life he would ardently prepare his sermons and then continue with reading the works of theologians and spiritual writers in the evenings. From a young age he was animated by a strong desire to "win over souls for our good Lord" as a priest and was supported by the confidence of the nearby pastor of Écully, who had no doubts about his vocation and provided him with a good part of his preparation. What an example of courage for those today who have the grace of being called to the priesthood!

The Depth of His Love for Christ and for Souls

4. The Curé of Ars is a model of priestly zeal for all shepherds of souls. The secret of his generosity is found without a doubt in *his love for God*, lived without limits as a constant response to the love manifested by *Christ crucified*.

It is upon this that he grounds his desire to do everything possible for the salvation of souls, redeemed by Christ at such a high price, and to lead them back to God's love. Let us recall one of the lapidary phrases whose secret the Curé grasped: "The priesthood is the love for the heart of Jesus." He always talked about this love in his sermons and catecheses: "O my God, I would rather die loving you than live a single moment without loving you. . . . I love you, O my divine Savior, because you were crucified for me . . . [and] because you keep me crucified for you."

Because of Christ, he sought to fully conform himself to the radical demands that Jesus proposes to the disciples he sends out on a mission in the Gospel: prayer, poverty, humility, self-renunciation, and voluntary penance. And, like Christ, he too felt a love for his sheep that led him to extreme pastoral dedication and self-sacrifice. Rarely was a priest so aware of his responsibilities, consumed by the desire to tear his flock away from the grip of sin and lukewarmness: "O my God, grant me the conversion of my parish: I will accept whatever suffering you wish for the rest of my life!"

Dear brother priests, nourished by the Second Vatican Council that happily included the consecration of priests in the framework of its pastoral mission, let us seek the dynamism of our pastoral zeal—along with St. John Mary Vianney—in the heart of Jesus and in his love for souls. If we do not draw from the same wellspring, our ministry risks bearing little fruit!

The Wonderful and Numerous Fruits of Our Ministry

5. In the case of the Curé of Ars, somewhat like Jesus in the Gospel, *the fruits were astonishing*. The Savior, to whom John Mary Vianney consecrated all his strength and all his heart, granted him souls in a certain sense. He entrusted them to him, and in overabundance.

First of all, *his parish*—which upon his arrival included only 230 people—would become profoundly transformed. It is a fact that there was significant indifference and very little religious practice among the people in that village. The bishop had prepared John Mary Vianney with the following words: "There is not much love for God in that parish: you will bring it to them." But in relatively short time, the Curé had become the pastor of a multitude from all over the region, well beyond his village, both from other parts of France and even from other countries. The number was roughly 80,000 in the year 1858! At times they had to wait many days before meeting him and confessing. What attracted them was not so much curiosity or even the justified renown of his miracles and extraordinary healings, which he would have preferred to keep secret, but much more: it was the idea of meeting a saint who was stunning because of his penitence, so close to God in prayer, extraordinary for his peace and humility amid popular success, and above all so perceptive in understanding the inner dispositions of souls and freeing them of their burdens, particularly in the confessional. Yes, God chose someone who might seem poor, weak, defenseless, and worthless to human eyes (see 1 Cor 1:27-29) as a model for priests. He graced him with his greatest of gifts as a guide and healer of souls.

While recognizing a unique grace granted to the Curé of Ars, do we not find here the sign of hope for today's priests who are suffering in a certain spiritual desert?

THE PRIMARY WORKS OF THE MINISTRY
OF THE CURÉ OF ARS

Various Apostolic Initiatives Aimed at the Essentials

6. John Mary Vianney dedicated himself in an essential way to the teaching of the faith and the purification of consciences, and these two ministries converged toward the Eucharist. Should we not see in this today the three dimensions of priestly pastoral service? Though the aim is certainly to bring the people of God together around the eucharistic mystery by means of catechesis and penance, other forms of apostolic contact are also necessary in accordance with the circumstances: at times it may be a simple presence silently witnessing to the faith in non-Christian contexts, perhaps over a period of many years; it might be remaining close to people, families, and their concerns; at times it may be a first announcement struggling to reawaken the faith of nonbelievers and lukewarm believers; it could also be witnessing to charity and justice together with lay Christians, making the faith more credible by putting it into practice. This leads to a whole series of activities or apostolic works that prepare or continue Christian preparation. The Curé of Ars himself took care to begin initiatives that corresponded to his time and to his parishioners. Nevertheless, all of his priestly activities were centered on the Eucharist, catechesis, and the Sacrament of Reconciliation.

The Sacrament of Reconciliation

7. What revealed the primary charism of the Curé of Ars and rightfully brought him renown was certainly his tireless dedication to the Sacrament of Penance. Today, it is good for such an example to lead us to give back to the ministry of reconciliation the importance it deserves, which was rightfully highlighted by the 1983 Synod of Bishops. Without the journey of conversion, penance, and asking of forgiveness that the ministers of the Church must tirelessly encourage and welcome, the much-desired renewal is destined to remain superficial and illusory.

The Curé of Ars was first and foremost concerned with teaching believers how to desire repentance. He emphasized the beauty of divine forgiveness. Were not his entire priestly life and all his efforts perhaps dedicated to the conversion of sinners? Well, it was primarily in the confessional that the mercy of God became manifest. He therefore had no

intention of leaving the penitents who came from all over and to whom
he often dedicated ten hours a day, and at times fifteen or even more. For
him, this was without a doubt the greatest of ascetic practices and a form
of "martyrdom": first of all physically, in the heat, in the cold, or in that
suffocating environment; and then morally, because he himself suffered
for the sins confessed and even more for a lack of contrition: "I weep for
the things you do not weep for." Along with such indifferent souls, whom
he welcomed as best he could and attempted to awaken to the love of
God, the Lord granted him the grace of reconciling great yet contrite
sinners and guiding those souls with an active desire toward perfection. It
was primarily here that God asked him to participate in redemption.

Today we have rediscovered, better than in the last century, the
community aspect of contrition, of preparation for forgiveness, and of
the action of grace after forgiveness. But sacramental forgiveness always
requires a personal encounter with Christ crucified through the mediation of his minister. Oftentimes, unfortunately, penitents do not fervently
crowd around the confessional as they did during the time of the Curé of
Ars. Now, the fact itself that so many of them seem to completely abstain
from confession is a sign of the urgent need to develop a whole pastoral
initiative for the Sacrament of Penance, continually bringing Christians
to rediscover the demands of a true relationship with God, the meaning
of sin by which we close ourselves to the Other and to others, the need
for conversion and receiving forgiveness as a gratuitous gift from God by
way of the Church, and finally the conditions that allow the sacrament to
be celebrated well, overcoming prejudices about it, false fears, and mere
habit. At the same time, such a situation requires us to remain highly
available for this ministry of forgiveness, ready to dedicate the necessary
time and attention. In fact, I would go even further: we need to give it
priority over other activities. In this way, believers will understand the
value we place on it, following the example of the Curé of Ars.

Of course, as I wrote in the post-synodal apostolic exhortation *Reconciliatio et Paenitentia* (*On Reconciliation and Penance in the Mission of the
Church Today*), reconciliation remains without a doubt the most difficult,
delicate, tiring, and demanding ministry, particularly when there are so
few priests. It also requires great personal qualities in the confessor and
above all an intense and sincere spiritual life; it is necessary for the priest
himself to make use of this sacrament frequently.

Always remain convinced of this, dear brother priests: this ministry of mercy is one of the most beautiful and consoling of all. It allows you to enlighten consciences, forgive them, give them back life in the name of the Lord Jesus, and be their healers and spiritual advisors; it remains "the irreplaceable manifestation and verification of the ministerial priesthood."

The Eucharist: Offering of the Mass, Communion, and Adoration

8. The Sacrament of Reconciliation and the Sacrament of the Eucharist are closely united to one another. Without a constantly renewed conversion and the acceptance of the sacramental grace of forgiveness, participation in the Eucharist would not come to its full redemptive efficacy. Just as Christ began his ministry saying, "Repent, and believe in the gospel" (Mk 1:15), so the Curé of Ars generally began each of his days with the ministry of forgiveness. But he was happy to guide his reconciled penitents toward the Eucharist.

The Eucharist was truly the center of his spiritual life and pastoral works. He would say, "All good works put together do not equal the sacrifice of the Mass because they are the work of men, whereas the Holy Mass is the work of God." It is here that the sacrifice on Calvary for the redemption of the world is made present. Obviously, the priest must unite the daily gift of himself to the sacrifice of the Mass: "A priest therefore does well to offer himself to God in sacrifice every morning!" "Holy Communion and the Holy Sacrifice of the Mass are the two most efficacious acts for obtaining the conversion of hearts." Moreover, for John Mary Vianney the Mass was the greatest joy and comfort of his priestly life. Despite the stream of penitents, he made a great effort to silently prepare himself for at least fifteen minutes before the Mass. He celebrated with meditative concentration, clearly expressing his adoration at the moments of the Consecration and Communion. He observed with realism that "the reason priests have become lax is that they no longer celebrate Mass with careful attention."

The Curé of Ars was particularly struck by the permanence of the Real Presence of Christ in the Eucharist. He would usually spend long hours in adoration before the tabernacle, before dawn or at dusk; he would often turn to it during his homilies and say, "He is there!" It is for this reason that he who was so frugal with his rectory yet would not hesitate to spend money on the beautification of the church. The valuable result was that his parishioners quickly acquired the habit of coming to pray before the Blessed Sacrament, discovering the wonder of the mystery of faith through the conduct of their Curé.

Regarding such a form of witnessing, let us think of what the Second Vatican Council tells us about priests today: "Their sacred ministry is primarily exercised in Eucharistic worship." And much more recently, the Extraordinary Synod (December 1985) reminds us that "the liturgy should promote the sense of the sacred and make it shine forth. It should be filled with reverence, adoration, and glorification of God. . . . The Eucharist is the source and summit of all Christian life."

My dear brother priests, the example of the Curé of Ars invites us to a serious examination of conscience. What place do we give to the celebration of the Mass in our daily lives? It was our first act as priests on the day of our ordination: has it remained the origin of our apostolic action and personal sanctification as it was then? How much care do we take in preparing ourselves for it? In celebrating it? In praying before the Blessed Sacrament? In guiding our flock? In turning our churches into the House of God, to which the divine presence may attract our contemporaries who all too often have the impression that the world is devoid of God?

Preaching and Catechesis

9. The Curé of Ars still considered it important not to neglect the ministry of the Word, which is absolutely necessary for preparing a person for faith and conversion. He even reached the point of saying, "Our Lord, who is truth itself, considers his Word no less than his Body." The time he dedicated to the diligent preparation of his Sunday homilies, particularly at the beginning, is well known. Later, he reached the point of expressing himself more spontaneously and with lively and clear conviction, using images and comparisons drawn from his daily experiences that were very striking to the faithful. Even his catecheses for children were an important part of his ministry, and adults would gladly join in with the children to take advantage of such unparalleled testimony flowing from the heart.

He had the courage to denounce evil in all its forms, without compromise, because the eternal salvation of his flock was at stake: "If a pastor remains silent though he sees God offended and souls in ruin, woe to him! If there is some disorder in his parish and he does not wish to be condemned, he must trample over his human sense of prudence and his fear of being disdained and hated." This responsibility was a cause of his anguish as a pastor. But usually "he preferred to show the beauties of virtue rather than the ugliness of vice," and if he recalled the sin—at times in tears—or the danger to a soul's salvation, he insisted on the tenderness of God even after an offense and on the happiness of being loved by God, being united to God, and living in his presence and for him.

My dear brother priests, you are thoroughly convinced of the importance of proclaiming the Gospel, which the Second Vatican Council declared first among all the functions of the priesthood. You struggle to reach our contemporaries—with all their hopes and uncertainties—through catechesis, preaching, and other forms of communication that even make use of the mass media in order to elicit and nourish their faith. Like the Curé of Ars and in accordance with the exhortation of the Council, dedicate yourselves to teaching the Word of God in itself, which calls all men and women to conversion and holiness.

THE IDENTITY OF PRIESTS

The Unique Ministry of Priests
10. St. John Mary Vianney offers an eloquent response to certain efforts to *dispute the identity of priests* that have emerged over the past twenty years. It now seems, however, that more balanced positions are being reached.

A priest must always and unshakably find the source of his identity in Christ the Priest. It is not the world that establishes his status in accordance with the needs or understandings of social roles; rather, a priest is marked by the seal of the Priesthood of Christ in order to participate in Christ's function as the one Mediator and Redeemer.

Precisely because of this fundamental connection, the vast field of service to souls lies open before the priest for their salvation in Christ and in the Church. It is a form of service that must be completely inspired by love of souls and likeness to Christ, who offers his life for them. God wills that all men and women be saved and that not one of these little ones be lost (see Mt 18:14). "A priest must always be prepared to respond to the needs of souls," the Curé of Ars once said. "[He] is not for himself; he is for you."

Priests are for the laypeople: they animate and sustain them in the exercise of the common priesthood of all the baptized, which was so well emphasized by the Second Vatican Council and which consists of turning one's life into a spiritual offering, giving witness to the Christian spirit in the family, taking on temporal commitments, and participating in the evangelization of our brothers and sisters. Nonetheless, the service of a priest is on another level. He is ordered toward acting in the name of Christ the Head; toward guiding men and women to the new life inaugurated by Christ; toward allowing them to participate in his mysteries of the Word, forgiveness, and the Bread of Life; toward calling them together into his Body; toward helping them to become formed from within and to live and act in accordance with God's plan of salvation. In summary, our identity as priests is made manifest in the "creative" unfurling of the love for souls communicated by Jesus Christ. Attempts to laicize priests are harmful to the Church.

This does not mean that priests can remain far removed from the human concerns of the laypeople: they must remain very close to them, like John Mary Vianney, but as priests, always in the perspective of salvation and advancement toward the Kingdom of God. They are the witnesses to and bestowers of a life different from earthly life.

It is essential for the Church that the identity of priests with its vertical dimension be safeguarded. The life and person of the Curé of Ars are a particularly enlightening and powerful example of it.

His Intimate Configuration to Christ and His Solidarity with Sinners

11. St. John Mary Vianney was effectively not fully satisfied with ritually carrying out the actions of his ministry. It was his very heart and life that he sought to conform to Christ.

Prayer was the soul of his life: silent, contemplative prayer, usually at the foot of the tabernacle in his church. Through Christ, his soul was opened to the Three Divine Persons to whom he would consign "his poor soul" in his last will and testament. "He maintained constant union with God in the midst of his very busy life." And he neglected neither the Divine Office nor the Rosary. He would spontaneously turn to the Virgin.

His *poverty* was extraordinary. He literally stripped himself for the poor, and he fled from honors. *Chastity* beamed through his gaze. He knew the price of purity to find "the source of love, which is God." For John Mary Vianney, obedience to Christ translated into obedience to the

Church and especially to his bishop. It was embodied in his acceptance of the difficult role of pastor, which often frightened him.

But the Gospel insists above all on *self-renunciation*, or the acceptance of the Cross. The Curé of Ars was presented with many crosses during the course of his ministry: calumnies by the people, misunderstandings by a vicar and fellow priests, contradictions, a mysterious struggle against the powers of hell, and at times even the temptation to despair in the midst of a dark night of the soul.

Nonetheless, accepting these trials without complaint was not sufficient for him: he practiced mortification, subjecting himself to constant fasting and much harsher forms of "reducing his body to servitude," as St. Paul says. But what needs to be seen clearly in this penance, which our time has unfortunately lost the habit of practicing, is the motivation behind it: love of God and the conversion of sinners. This is how he questioned a discouraged brother priest: "You have prayed . . . you have wailed . . . but have you fasted, have you kept vigil?" This brings us to Jesus' warning to the Apostles: "This kind [of evil spirit] does not come out except by prayer and fasting" (Mt 17:21).

John Mary Vianney definitively sanctified himself in order to better sanctify others. Of course, conversion remains a secret of the heart, free to make its decision, and a secret of God's grace. With his ministry, a priest can only enlighten the person, guide him to the confessional, and give him the sacraments. These sacraments are indeed acts of Christ, and their efficacy is not diminished by the imperfection or unworthiness of the minister. But the result also depends on the disposition of the recipient, and that disposition is powerfully aided by the personal holiness of the priest, by his proven witness, and also by the mysterious exchange of merits in the Communion of Saints. St. Paul said, "In my flesh I am filling up what is lacking in the afflictions of Christ on behalf of his body, which is the church" (Col 1:24). Not only through his prayer, but also through the sacrifice of his entire life, John Mary Vianney sought in a certain sense to wrench the graces of conversion from God's hands. He sought to love God for those who did not love him, and even to fulfill most of the penances for those who did not do them. He was truly a pastor united to his sinful people.

My dear brother priests, let us not fear this personal involvement—marked by asceticism and inspired by love—that God asks of us in order to best exercise our priesthood. Let us remind ourselves of the recent reflections of the Synodal Fathers: "It seems that in the present difficulties God wishes to more profoundly teach us the value, importance, and central role of the Cross of Jesus Christ." In priests, Christ relives his Passion for the sake of souls. Let us give thanks to God, who allows us to participate in the Redemption of our heart and of our flesh!

For all these reasons, St. John Mary Vianney never ceases to be an ever living, ever present witness to the truth of the priestly vocation and priestly service. May we recall the convincing tone in which he spoke of the greatness of priests and their absolute necessity. Priests, those preparing for the priesthood, and those who will be called to it must fix their eyes upon his example and follow it. All believers will themselves better understand the mystery of the priesthood of their priests thanks to him. *No, the figure of the Curé of Ars will never wane!*

Conclusion for Holy Thursday

12. Dear brothers, may these reflections revive in you the joy of being priests and the desire to be so ever more profoundly! The witness of the Curé of Ars still contains many other riches to explore.

I send you this meditation, dear brothers, for the solemnity of Holy Thursday. In each of our diocesan communities, we will gather on this birthday of our priesthood to renew the grace of the Sacrament of Holy Orders and to reinvigorate the love that characterizes our vocation.

Let us listen to Christ, who repeats to us what he told the Apostles: "No one has greater love than this, to lay down one's life for one's friends. . . . I no longer call you slaves . . . I have called you friends" (Jn 15:13-15).

We renew our priestly commitments as priests and bishops before he who manifests Love in its fullness.

Let us pray for one another, each for his brothers, and each for all.

Let us ask the Eternal Priest that the memory of the Curé of Ars may help us revive our zeal to serve him.

Let us beseech the Holy Spirit to call many more priests of the character and holiness of the Curé of Ars to serve the Church: our time has great need of them as well, and he is no less capable of bringing those vocations to blossom.

And we entrust our priesthood to the Virgin Mary, Mother of Priests, to whom John Mary Vianney turned ceaselessly with tender affection and total trust. For him, this was yet another reason to be thankful. "Jesus Christ," he said, "after having given us everything he could give, still wished to make us the heirs to his most precious possession: his Blessed Mother."

Thoughts By and About the Holy Curé of Ars

Voluntary Poverty

THE DOORWAY OF WEALTH

- "Oh, how those poor pastors whose rectories are adorned with palace furniture should feel sorry for themselves."
- "The doorway through which pride enters most easily is the doorway of wealth."
- "An old cassock goes well with a nice chasuble."
- "A bit of beans, sometimes two eggs, and a little meat when he was very tired. In less than ten minutes he had finished eating."
- "I have noticed that those who have some income are always complaining. They are always missing something. Those who have nothing always want for nothing."
- "We would like to go to heaven, but with all of our comforts: without inconveniencing ourselves about anything."
- "Whenever I am worried about Providence, the Lord punishes me for my worries by sending me unforeseen assistance."

THE NEED FOR MONEY

- "People think I have no need for money. And yet the feast of St. Martin is drawing near: we have more than thirty rents to pay."
- "He sold the books of his library in order to help the poor in his parish."
- When he was granted a mozzetta as an honorary canon, he said, "I would have preferred that they give me something for the poor of my parish."
- "My secret is quite simple: give everything away and do not put anything aside [for yourself]."
- "I have never seen anyone fall into ruin from having done good works."
- Limitless generosity and prudence: "We have to be very careful of debts."

The Poor Who Come to Ask

- "How fortunate we are that the poor come to us. If they did not come we would have to go looking, and we do not always have the time."
- "I only ever begged for alms once in my life, and I did not like it. It was then that I understood how it is better to give than to receive."
- "There are those who say, 'They will use the money inappropriately.' They will be judged by God on the use they make of it, and you will be judged on whether you gave it or not."
- "There are those who say to the poor who appear to be in good health, 'You are a mountain of a man: you could work, you are young, and you have strong arms!' But you do not know the reason in God's plan that this poor man is begging for food. You expose yourselves to the danger of murmuring against the will of God."
- He did not give indiscriminately to everyone in the same way; he gave much to those who were truly in need, and to the ordinary poor he gave less.
- "We must never disdain the poor, because this disdain reflects back onto God."
- He understood that you must reach the heart through the stomach.
- "Charity is not accomplished by money alone."
- "A small act of corporal almsgiving allows spiritual almsgiving to get through."

Faithful to Your Sublime Vocation Like the Curé of Ars, May You Always Remain Totally Willing to Serve the Gospel

Spiritual Retreat for Priests, Deacons, and Seminarians

Pope John Paul II traveled in pilgrimage to France in October 1986. On October 6, he stopped in Ars; after visiting the basilica dedicated to St. John Mary Vianney, the Pope presided over a spiritual retreat for priests, deacons, and seminarians. The retreat consisted of three successive stages, during which the Holy Father offered the following meditations.

I. THE MORE THE CHRISTIAN PEOPLE BECOME AWARE OF THEIR PROPER DIGNITY, THE MORE THEY FEEL THE NEED FOR PRIESTS WHO ARE TRULY PRIESTS

First Reading

A reading from the holy Gospel according to John (20:19-23)

On the evening of that first day of the week,
when the doors were locked, where the disciples were,
for fear of the Jews,
Jesus came and stood in their midst

and said to them, "Peace be with you."
When he had said this, he showed them his hands and his side.
The disciples rejoiced when they saw the Lord.
Jesus said to them again, "Peace be with you.
As the Father has sent me, so I send you."
And when he had said this, he breathed on them and said to
    them,
"Receive the Holy Spirit.
Whose sins you forgive are forgiven them,
and whose sins you retain are retained."

The Gospel of the Lord.

1. "As the Father has sent me, so I send you. . . . Receive the holy Spirit."

Dear brothers, *it is Christ who chooses us and sends us*, just as he was sent by the Father, and who shares the Holy Spirit with us. Our priesthood is rooted in the missions of the Divine Persons, in their reciprocal giving in the heart of the Holy Trinity. "The grace of the Holy Spirit . . . continues to be transmitted in Episcopal Ordination. The bishops in turn by the Sacrament of Orders render the sacred ministers sharers in this spiritual gift" (John Paul II, *Dominum et Vivificantem*, no. 25). Priests as well as deacons participate in this grace.

Our mission is a *mission of salvation*. "God did not send his Son into the world to condemn the world, but that the world might be saved through him" (Jn 3:17). Jesus preached the Good News of the Kingdom; he chose and instructed his Apostles; he fulfilled the work of redemption through the Cross and Resurrection; following the Apostles, we are united to his work of salvation in a unique way, for the purpose of making it present and efficacious everywhere in the world. St. John Mary Vianney even said, "Without priests, the Passion and death of our Lord would be for nothing. It is priests who continue the work of redemption on earth."

What we must come to fulfill then is not *our work*: it is the Father's design, and it is the Son's work of salvation. The Holy Spirit makes use of our spirit, our mouth, and our hands. In a particular way, it is our task to ceaselessly proclaim the Word and to evangelize: to translate it in a way that reaches hearts, without changing or diminishing it; and to repeat Jesus' gesture of offering at the Last Supper and his gestures of forgiveness to sinners.

2. It is not merely a task that we have received, or a qualified function to be carried out in service of the People of God. Some may speak of the priesthood as a job or a function, including the function of presiding over the eucharistic banquet. But we cannot be reduced to being its functionaries.

This is first of all because *it is within our very being* that we are signed through ordination with a unique character that configures us to Christ the Priest in order to make us capable of acting in the name of Christ the Head in person. Of course, we are occupied in the midst of all the people and we remain close to them, as St. Augustine said, as "Christians in their midst." But we are "set aside," fully consecrated to the work of salvation. "Inasmuch as it is connected with the episcopal order, the priestly office shares in the authority by which Christ Himself builds up, sanctifies, and rules His Body" (Second Vatican Council, *Presbyterorum Ordinis*, no. 2). It is the Second Vatican Council that reminds us of this.

We are at the same time in the midst of the Christian assembly and before it, indicating that the initiative of sanctification comes from God, the Head of the Body, and that the Church receives it. Sent in the name of Christ, we have been sanctified by him for a specific purpose: it remains in us and profoundly touches our being as baptized Christians.

The Curé of Ars had some very weighty words regarding this topic: "God puts a priest on the earth as another mediator between the Lord and the poor sinner." Today we would say that he participates in a unique way in the mission of the one Mediator, Jesus Christ.

This leads to a consequence for *our life* in everyday contexts. As Fr. Chevrier has said, we are disciples embodying the mysteries of Christ's life. It is therefore normal that we should continuously seek to conform ourselves to Christ—on whose behalf we are ministers—not only in the actions of our ministry, but also in our thoughts, the attachments of our hearts, and our conduct. This obviously presupposes a true intimacy with Christ in prayer. Our whole person and our entire life refer back to Christ: "Imitate what you celebrate." All the baptized are called to holiness, but our consecration and mission invest us with a particular duty to work toward it, whether we are secular or religious clergy, through the inherent treasures of our priesthood and the demands of our ministry in the midst of the People of God.

Of course, the sacraments owe their efficacy to Christ and not to our office. We are his poor and humble instruments who should not attribute to ourselves the merit of the graces transmitted, yet we are responsible instruments, and so a soul becomes better prepared to cooperate with that grace through the holiness of the minister.

It is precisely in the Curé of Ars that we see a priest who was not content to merely go through the external motions of the redemption; he participated in it with his very being, in his love of Christ, in constant prayer, in the offering of his trials and voluntary mortifications. I already said as much to priests at Notre Dame in Paris on May 30, 1980: "The Curé of Ars remains an unparalleled model for all nations both in terms of the fulfillment of the ministry and the holiness of the minister."

3. This means telling you, dear friends, that we can rightfully admire the wonder of the ministerial priesthood as well as the religious vocation, because there is a certain relationship between the two. You know the words of the Curé of Ars: "What an incredible thing it is to be a priest! If he were to fully grasp it, his life could not withstand it."

Indeed, how wonderful it is to exercise our threefold priestly mission as bishops and priests, which is so essential to the Church, by

- Proclaiming the Good News: bringing Jesus Christ to others; entering into an authentic relationship with him; guarding the authenticity and accuracy of the faith so that it does not give way or become changed or hardened; and maintaining the evangelical impetus of the Church by encouraging and teaching a spirit of apostolate.
- Dispensing the mysteries of God: making them authentically present, in particular the Paschal Mystery through the Eucharist and forgiveness; and allowing the baptized to have access to it and preparing them for it. Laypeople can never be assigned to such ministries; priestly ordination allowing action in the name of Christ the Head is necessary.
- Shepherding the flock by building and maintaining communion among Christians, in the communities entrusted to us, together with the other diocesan communities and in union with the Successor of Peter. Before becoming specialized based on his personal competencies and in agreement with his bishop, a priest is in fact a minister for the community: in a Christian community that often risks falling apart or closing itself off, he ensures both the unity of the family of God

and its openness at the same time. His priesthood confers on him the authority to guide the priestly people.

4. The *specific identity of priests* thus becomes clearer. In fact, after the debates over the past twenty years, it is now ever less frequently questioned. But the scant number of priests and priestly ordinations in many nations may lead some laypeople and even priests to surrender to this dearth under the pretext that the role of the laypeople has become better understood and put into practice.

It is true that the Council felicitously resituated the ministerial priesthood in the perspective of the apostolic mission of the People of God. It prevented turning it into advancement as "an end in itself," detached from the people. It highlighted the fundamental importance of proclaiming the Word, which prepares the ground for faith and then for the sacraments. It better articulated the relationship between the priesthood of priests and the priesthood of bishops, and it illustrated the relationship of the priesthood to the ordained ministry of deacons and the common priesthood of all the baptized through which they can and should have access to the treasures of grace (filial adoption, the life of Christ, the Holy Spirit, the sacraments, etc.), make their lives a spiritual offering, give witness as disciples of Christ in the world, and take on their role in the apostolate and service of the Church.

Yet in order to fully exercise this prophetic, priestly, and kingly office, the baptized are in need of the ministerial priesthood through which the gift of divine life received in Christ, the Head of the entire Body, is transmitted to them in a privileged and tangible way. The more the people are truly Christian and become aware of their position and properly active role in the Church, the more they feel the need for priests who are truly priests. And the same is true for regions that have abandoned Christianity and social circles that have become isolated from the Church. Laypeople and priests cannot give up when they see the number of priestly vocations and ordinations reduced to their current levels in many dioceses. This surrender would be a bad sign for the life of the Christian people, and it would be dangerous for its future and mission. And it would be a doubtful response to organize Christian communities as though they could do without the priestly ministry, under the pretext of realistically confronting the impending situation. Let us instead ask ourselves if we are doing everything possible to reinvigorate the Christian people's awareness of the beauty and necessity of the priesthood and to reawaken vocations, encouraging them and bringing them to maturity. I am happy to know that your vocations services are developing new initiatives to once again present the call. Let us never grow weary of praying and asking for prayers that the Master of the harvest may send more laborers.

My dear brother priests, let us remain modest and humble, for this is a grace of the Lord we have received in order to serve others, a grace of which we will never be truly worthy. The Curé of Ars used to say, "A priest is not for himself; he is for you." Nonetheless, like him, we must never stop admiring the grandeur of our priesthood and giving thanks at all times. And may you, dear seminarians, aspire ever more in joy and hope to this highest of services to the Lord and his Church!

Prayer

Lord,
like the apostle Peter,
we have felt
in the depths of our life
the call to leave safe shores,
to travel afar,
to leave behind the nets of human pursuits.
Through the Church,
you have called and consecrated us,
anointed by your Spirit
and sent before you
to act in your name,
serving all the members
of the People of God,
so that they may ever more clearly receive
your message and your divine life.
Make us able to ceaselessly dwell
in the action of grace
and carefully conform our entire life
to the sanctity of this ministry.
You who live with the Father and the Holy Spirit,
forever and ever.
Amen.

II. Convert, Heal, and Save:
Three Key Words for Our Mission

Second Reading (A)

A reading from the first Letter of St. Paul to the Corinthians
(9:16-23)

Brothers and sisters:
If I preach the gospel, this is no reason for me to boast,
for an obligation has been imposed on me,
and woe to me if I do not preach it!
If I do so willingly, I have a recompense,
but if unwillingly, then I have been entrusted with a
    stewardship.
What then is my recompense?
That, when I preach,
I offer the gospel free of charge
so as not to make full use of my right in the gospel.

Although I am free in regard to all,
I have made myself a slave to all
so as to win over as many as possible.
To the weak I became weak, to win over the weak.
I have become all things to all, to save at least some.
All this I do for the sake of the gospel,
so that I too may have a share in it.

The word of the Lord.

Second Reading (B)

A reading from the second Letter of St. Paul to the Corinthians
(5:14–6:2)

Brothers and sisters:
The love of Christ impels us,
once we have come to the conviction that one died for all;
therefore, all have died.

He indeed died for all,
so that those who live might no longer live for themselves
but for him who for their sake died and was raised.

Consequently, from now on we regard no one according to the
    flesh;
even if we once knew Christ according to the flesh,
yet now we know him so no longer.
So whoever is in Christ is a new creation:
the old things have passed away;
behold, new things have come.
And all this is from God,
who has reconciled us to himself through Christ
and given us the ministry of reconciliation,
namely, God was reconciling the world to himself in Christ,
not counting their trespasses against them
and entrusting to us the message of reconciliation.
So we are ambassadors for Christ,
as if God were appealing through us.
We implore you on behalf of Christ,
be reconciled to God.
For our sake he made him to be sin who did not know sin,
so that we might become the righteousness of God in him.

Working together, then,
we appeal to you not to receive the grace of God in vain.
For he says:

In an acceptable time I heard you,
and on the day of salvation I helped you.

Behold, now is a very acceptable time;
behold, now is the day of salvation.

The word of the Lord.

5. "I have become all things to all, to save at least some."
    The word "salvation" was frequently on the lips of the Curé of Ars.
What did it mean for him? Being saved means being freed from sin, which

distances us from God, hardens our hearts, and risks separating us from God's love forever, which is the most atrocious fate. Being saved is living united to God; it is seeing God. Being saved is also being reintroduced to true communion with others, because many times our sins involve offending love of neighbor, justice, truth, and respect for our goods, our bodies, and our human rights; all of these are contrary to the will of God. And there is a profound solidarity between all the members of the Body of Christ: we cannot love him if we do not love our neighbor. Salvation therefore allows us to recover a filial relationship with God and a fraternal relationship with others.

Christ's *redemption* opened the possibility of salvation to all. Priests cooperate in redemption and prepare souls for it by preaching conversion and offering forgiveness. It was for their salvation that the Curé of Ars desired to become a priest: announcing his vocation at eighteen years of age, he affirmed his wish "to win over souls for our good Lord," reflecting St. Paul's aim "to win over as many as possible." It is for this reason that John Mary Vianney gave himself over to his last drop of strength and accepted doing penances, as if he were wrenching the graces of conversion from the hands of God. He feared and wept for their salvation. And when he was tempted to flee from his burdensome charge as pastor, he returned for the salvation of his parishioners. We hear from St. Paul that "the love of Christ impels us . . . now is the day of salvation." "The priesthood," John Mary Vianney also said, "is the love of the heart of Jesus."

Dear brother priests, many of our contemporaries seem to have become indifferent to the salvation of their souls. Are we sufficiently concerned about this loss of faith, or do we surrender?

Of course, today we are right to insist on the love of God, who sent his Son to save and not to condemn. We are right to emphasize love rather than worry and fear. In fact, this is also what the Curé of Ars did.

Furthermore, men and women are free to adhere to faith and salvation or not; they loudly claim this freedom, and the Church also desires their steps to be free from external pressures other than the moral duty of each person to seek and adhere to truth and to act in accordance with his or her conscience.

Ultimately, God himself is free from his gifts. Conversion is a grace. In the encyclical letter *Dominum et Vivificantem*, I explained that only the Holy Spirit brings us to understand the gravity of sin and the tragedy of losing our sense of God and grants us the desire for conversion.

But our love for others cannot surrender to the fact that they deprive themselves of salvation. We have a direct impact on the conversion of souls and are still responsible for the proclamation of the faith—the complete faith—and its demands. We must invite our faithful to conversion and holiness and speak the truth, not only informing them of the sacraments that restore them to God's grace, but recommending the sacraments and instilling a desire for them! The Curé of Ars considered this a difficult but necessary ministry: "If a shepherd remains silent though he sees God offended and souls misled, woe to him!" We know what care he took in preparing his Sunday homilies and his catecheses and what courage he showed in reminding his people of the demands of the Gospel, denouncing sin, and inviting them to make amends for the wrongs committed.

Convert, heal, and save: these are the three key words for our mission. The Curé of Ars proved himself truly united to his sinful people; he did everything possible to wrench those souls away from their sins and lukewarmness and bring them back to love. He prayed, "O my God, grant me the conversion of my parish: I will accept whatever suffering you wish for the rest of my life!" It has been said that he had "a passionate view of salvation"; perhaps the influence of Jansenism led to severe expressions and tones, but he was able to overcome its exaggerated rigor. He instead preferred insisting on the attractive side of virtue and on God's mercy, through which our sins become "like grains of sand." He showed the tenderness of our offended God. His ardent appeals on the importance of salvation and the urgent need for conversion fit in perfectly with the line of appeals by the prophets, Jesus, St. Paul, and St. Augustine. He feared that priests "would become apathetic" by becoming accustomed to the indifference of their people. How can we ignore his warning today?

6. "Be reconciled to God."

This phrase in St. Paul's letter precisely defines the ministry of St. John Mary Vianney. He is known throughout the world as a priest who would confess for up to ten or fifteen hours or more every day, and he continued doing this up until the last five days before his death. We certainly do not have to literally apply his schedule as a confessor to our own priestly lives, but his attitude and motivation nevertheless face us with powerful questions.

Offering pardon to contrite souls was the essential core of his ministry of salvation, even at the price of an exertion that never ceases to astound us. Do we afford the same importance to the Sacrament of Reconciliation? Are we ready to dedicate time to it? Do we adequately teach our faithful to desire it and how to prepare themselves for it? Do we sufficiently commit ourselves to finding the practical means of offering them the real possibility of confession in our cities and towns? Do we seek to renew the celebration of the sacrament in conformity with the Church's suggestions (Gospel accompaniment, periodically guaranteed community preparation, etc.), never forgetting the need for personal confession at least for grave sins? Do we try to clarify that the confession of such grave sins is a necessary condition for participating in the Eucharist and for properly celebrating the Sacrament of Marriage? Do we appreciate the marvelous occasion we therefore have to form consciences and guide souls toward spiritual growth?

Dear friends, I know that after a difficult period many priests, together with their bishops, have tried to recover. I encourage you to do so with all my heart. This was the topic of the post-synodal document *On Reconciliation and Penance in the Mission of the Church Today* (*Reconciliatio et Paenitentia*).

I also know that you face many difficulties, including the shortage of priests and above all the estrangement of the faithful from the Sacrament of Penance. You say, "They have no longer been coming to confession for some time now." This is exactly the problem! Does this not perhaps reveal a lack of faith, of the sense of sin, and of the meaning of the mediation of Christ and his Church, as well as disdain for a practice whose habit-related distortions are the only thing they remember?

We recall that the bishop of the Curé of Ars told him, "There is not much love of God in this parish; you will bring it to them." And the holy Curé also found dispassionate penitents. Nevertheless, thanks to his priestly bearing and holiness, a group of considerable size grasped the importance of the sacrament of forgiveness. What was the secret by which he attracted both believers and nonbelievers, saints and sinners? The Curé of Ars, who so harshly condemned sin in certain sermons, was actually very merciful—like Jesus—in meeting with each individual sinner. Fr. Monnin said that he was a "hearth of tenderness and mercy." He burned with the mercy of Christ.

This is a question regarding a highly important aspect of evangelization. Beginning on Easter evening, the Apostles are sent to forgive sins.

The gift of the Holy Spirit is connected to this power. And the book of the Acts of the Apostles continually returns to the forgiveness of sins as a new grace. It is the guiding reason behind apostolic preaching: "Be reconciled."

These words are also directed to us, dear friends. Are we faithful in personally accepting forgiveness through the mediation of another priest?

7. It is *to the Eucharist* that John Mary Vianney wished to lead his contrite faithful. You know the central place of the Mass in each of his days and the careful attention with which he prepared for and celebrated it. He was well aware that the renewal of Christ's *sacrifice* is the source of the graces of conversion. He also insisted on *Communion*, inviting those who were duly prepared to receive it more frequently, which was contrary to the pastoral approach of the time. You also know that the *Real Presence* of Christ in the Eucharist enthralled him both during and outside of Mass. He could so often be found in adoration at the foot of the tabernacle! And his poor parishioners never delayed to come themselves to greet and adore Christ in the Blessed Sacrament.

The Council has allowed us to renew our eucharistic celebrations, to open them to the participation of the community, and to render them lively, expressive, and easy to follow. I think that the Curé of Ars would rejoice in this. Nevertheless, we realize that not everything has proceeded down the right path. *The significant reduction of religious worship*, which is due to many factors I do not wish to analyze here, is highly disconcerting. Our faithful need to recover their place in Christian life. This was one of the fundamental catechetical teachings of the Curé of Ars. The dignity of the celebration and meditative recollection are values that have not always been respected. The Curé of Ars considered it very important to create an atmosphere of prayer in his church that was accessible to the people and suitable to fostering adoration even outside of Mass. Who would not wish to foster this appreciation for silent prayer and this sense of inner life in our churches?

Yet another thing strikes us: the Curé of Ars worked extensively to reestablish the *sense of Sunday* in order to free mothers and housemaids from their chores for the eucharistic encounter. I urge you to continue promoting the Christian meaning of Sunday.

I will leave you to meditate upon this grace the Lord grants us of forgiving sins in his name and offering his Body as nourishment for our brothers and sisters. "Save with Christ!"

Prayer

Lord Jesus Christ,
who gave your life
so that all could be saved
and have life in abundance,
preserve in us the desire for the salvation
of all those you have entrusted
to our ministry.
Renew our readiness
to offer them reconciliation with God
and with their brothers and sisters,
like St. Paul and St. John Mary Vianney.
We give you thanks
for your Body and your Blood
that you allow us to offer each day
for the salvation of the world,
to receive in ourselves,
to give to our brothers and sisters,
and to worship in our churches.
Do not allow our hearts
to become accustomed to this gift:
grant that we may see
your extreme Love in it
as the Holy Curé of Ars did.
You who reign with the Father and the Holy Spirit
forever and ever.
Amen.

III. Celibacy, True Poverty, Obedience, Asceticism, and Acceptance of Trials: Means for Living the Joy of the Priesthood

Third Reading

A reading from the second Letter of St. Paul to the Corinthians
(4:1-15)

Therefore, since we have this ministry through the mercy shown
    us,
we are not discouraged.
And even though our Gospel is veiled,
it is veiled for those who are perishing,
in whose case the god of this age
has blinded the minds of the unbelievers,
so that they may not see the light of the Gospel
of the glory of Christ, who is the image of God.
For we do not preach ourselves but Jesus Christ as Lord,
and ourselves as your slaves for the sake of Jesus.
For God who said, *Let light shine out of darkness,*
has shone in our hearts to bring to light
the knowledge of the glory of God
on the face of Jesus Christ.
We hold this treasure in earthen vessels,
that the surpassing power may be of God and not from us.
We are afflicted in every way, but not constrained;
perplexed, but not driven to despair;
persecuted, but not abandoned;
struck down, but not destroyed;
always carrying about in the Body the dying of Jesus,
so that the life of Jesus may also be manifested in our body.
For we who live are constantly being given up to death
for the sake of Jesus,
so that the life of Jesus may be manifested in our mortal flesh.

So death is at work in us, but life in you.
Since, then, we have the same spirit of faith,
according to what is written, "I believed, therefore I spoke,"
we too believe and therefore speak,
knowing that the one who raised the Lord Jesus
will raise us also with Jesus
and place us with you in his presence.
Everything indeed is for you,
so that the grace bestowed in abundance on more and more
  people
may cause the thanksgiving to overflow for the glory of God.

The word of the Lord.

8. "We hold this treasure in earthen vessels, that the surpassing power may be of God and not from us."

My dear brother priests, it was necessary for us to meditate above all on the magnificence of the priesthood, on the "surpassing power" of salvation that God entrusts to us. But how can we ignore the tribulations of the ministry that St. Paul himself experienced? How can we not recognize the weaknesses of our "earthen vessels"? I would like to help you live through those tribulations with hope and encourage your efforts at becoming stronger. The Curé of Ars would say, "Do not be frightened by your burden, for our Lord bears it with you."

Though he faithfully serves only Jesus Christ, the challenges for an apostle can come *from the outside*. He is subjected to mockery, calumny, and obstacles to his freedom; he also comes to be, as St. Paul says, "afflicted in every way," "persecuted," and "struck down." In some nations, how many Christians and how many priests are suffering these persecutions in silence? They often stir up and purify the faith of the people as a result. But what a trial! And what an obstacle to their ministry! We remain united with these brothers of ours under trial.

There are different challenges in the Western nations. You encounter a widespread spirit of criticism, unbelief, secularization, and even atheism, or simply a closure that limits itself to materialistic concerns, and the message you seek to bring in the name of Christ and his Church becomes quickly relativized or rejected. Already in the 1950s, Cardinal Suhard had accurately described the sign of contradiction that a priest becomes in a society that fears his message and classifies him as either a utopist or someone living in the past. Since that time, priests have become far less numerous and their average age has risen in many dioceses. This age pyramid sometimes makes the integration of younger priests difficult.

Discouragement can also find fuel in our mentality as priests; some may allow themselves to be overcome by melancholy and bitterness in the face of unsuccessful efforts or endless debates; there is sometimes a stiffening due to ideologies foreign to the Christian and priestly spirit; or sometimes a spirit of systematic distrust toward Rome may develop. All of this has weighed and still weighs upon the activity of priests. I have the impression that the young people are less bound by this mentality. I encourage them, and I also invite them to appreciate the prior generations of tried and true priests: they have carried the weight of their daily activities and burdensome adversities of the times in the midst of many changes, and they have very often carried out their work with an evangelical spirit.

Lastly, each of you faces your own *personal challenges*: health, loneliness, family concerns, and the temptations of the world that enter you, stirring at times a great sense of spiritual poverty if not of humiliating weakness. Let us offer this fragility of our "earthen vessels" to God.

It is good for us to know that the Curé of Ars also experienced many trials: his body battered by the labors of his ministry and his fasting, the misunderstandings and calumnies of his parishioners, the critical suspicion and jealousy of his fellow priests, and certain more mysterious spiritual trials: a certain "supernatural melancholy," as Fr. Monnin says, a certain spiritual desolation, anxiety for his own salvation, a relentless struggle against the spirit of evil, and a certain lack of clarity.

Generous and spiritual souls are rarely without such trials. Nevertheless, despite his heightened sensitivity, the Curé of Ars never appeared discouraged. He resisted these temptations.

9. You, too, will therefore know the journey of salvation and the means for restoring yourselves.

I would first of all say this: a spiritual renewal.

How can we bring an end to the spiritual crisis of our time if we ourselves do not take advantage of that profound and constant union with the Lord that we are here to serve? We find an unparalleled guide in the

Curé of Ars. He said that "a priest is first and foremost a man of prayer . . . the intimate union that we need with God is meditation and prayer."

It is not without reason that our spiritual directors have insisted on time for daily prayer carried out gratuitously in the presence of the Lord, daily reading of the Word of God, adoration and petition in the name of the Church through the Liturgy of the Hours, daily celebration of the Eucharist, and Marian prayer. What admiration the Curé of Ars had for the Blessed Virgin, and what trust in her! He called her "my first love," saying that "we need only turn to her for our prayers to be granted!"

I am also thinking of regular time for retreats, allowing the Spirit of God the possibility to enter us, to "check on us," and to help us discern the essential core of our vocation.

The daily encounter with human tragedy and beauty in our ministry should evidently be incorporated into our prayer; it can nourish it, provided we bring everything before the Lord "for his glory."

All of our priestly duties acquire new meaning in light of this spiritual vitality, including

- Celibacy, the sign of our limitless availability to Christ and others
- True poverty, which is participation in the life of the poor Christ and the conditions of the poor
- Obedience, which translates our service in the Church
- Asceticism, which is necessary for every person's life, starting with the daily fulfillment of the duties of the ministry
- Acceptance of trials that unexpectedly arise and voluntary mortifications offered with love for the salvation of souls: the Curé of Ars lived out the Lord's word that some evil spirits can only be cast out by fasting and prayer (see Mt 17:21).

But, you might ask, where can we find the energy to do all of this? We are certainly not exonerated from being men of courage. But the yoke is easy and the burden light (see Mt 11:30) if our courage is supported by the faith that the Lord will not abandon those who trust in him, for "God is greater than our hearts" (1 Jn 3:20).

And on top of this, we will find joy: the emaciated countenance of the Curé of Ars always seemed to have a smile!

10. "To the weak I became weak. . . . I have become all things to all."

The priestly ministry therefore becomes the daily grounds for our sanctification when lived in a state of union with God. Jesus prayed to his Father on behalf of the Apostles in these words: "I do not ask that you take them out of the world but that you keep them from the evil one" (Jn 17:15). The Second Vatican Council recommended that priests never be disconnected and removed from the real existence and living conditions of their flock. This attitude of welcoming, listening, understanding, and sharing is always necessary for evangelization to be audible and credible. Fr. Chevrier made himself a poor man among the poor; similarly, it is necessary to enter into the mentalities of new evangelization contexts, whether rich or poor, learned or not. Through you, it is essential to preserve the missionary zeal of the oldest among you for the world today. But precisely for this reason, as the Council also says, priests will not forget that they are the ministers of a life distinct from earthly life, and that they should not model themselves on the world today but thoroughly examine themselves in the light of the Gospel. They should not even call into question the temporal or political choices of their faithful—even legitimate ones—so that their ministry may remain open to all and clearly directed toward the Kingdom of God.

11. The spiritual and apostolic qualities of tomorrow's priests are formed today, and I cannot neglect to remind you of *this formation*.

Dear seminarians, it is a joy for me to see you all together here! In greeting you, I am greeting those who ensure new clergy to replace the aging and dying clergy. Although you are still the small flock of the Gospel, I am filled with hope in seeing you. And I am counting on your joy in consecrating your lives to encourage many more candidates. I believe you are also ready to accept the demands of this life of service.

Many of you are entering the seminary at a more advanced age than in the past, usually after work and study experiences. Nevertheless, a survey has recently shown that you thought about the priesthood already before the age of thirteen. Accept the conditions for the discernment and maturation of your vocation. If God is calling you, and if the Church confirms it, do not let yourselves be discouraged by the trials of the journey. I think many of you are aware of the countless challenges that the young John Mary Vianney faced in order to become a priest: a lack of education and contact with cultured people, a delay caused by the French Revolution, the need to work on the farm, the distracting adventure of military service, and above all difficulties in learning Latin, a poor memory, hesitation on the part of the seminary directors, and a solitary ordination later in life in an occupied country. Of course, he benefited from various graces, such as a Christian family environment and the affectionate and firm assistance of Abbot Balley of Écully. Yet his journey toward the priesthood can encourage all those facing trials in bringing their vocation to maturity.

Your seminaries should be capable of accepting various sensibilities in the context of great reciprocal respect. Generous souls should not be inhibited based on the fears of others, nor should they be judged *a priori*. The link to the bishop is essential, and the accompaniment of a personal spiritual director and the judgment of a team of educators are a guarantee of a vocation. *You cannot conquer the priesthood*: you are called by those who judge you fit for it in the name of the bishop. I hope your seminaries prepare you as best they can for the priestly life we have continuously discussed today. Theology must be approached with the most complete initiation to the mystery of salvation possible, and consequently with a perspective that is simultaneously intellectual, scientific, and spiritual. Listening to the Word of God must be the highest priority in your seminaries, and formation in the spiritual life through appropriate dialogues and diligent readings is clearly essential. At the same time, you should fulfill the experience of fraternal community life and profound liturgical and personal prayer as I had mentioned regarding spiritual renewal. There is also a place for a certain learning of the ministry: how to understand today's world as it is and how to draw it closer through pastoral dialogue, which is a dialogue of salvation. On the threshold of priestly life, you should be open to the various pastoral duties necessary in a diocese and be available to accept the assignment entrusted to you.

All of these demands of seminary life, which many students fortunately seem to desire now, constitute a major responsibility for directors and professors. I pray that the Lord may assist them in this fundamental service to the Church.

12. As far as you *priests* are concerned, you are also in need of intellectual reinvigoration and stronger community support.

You understand the need for intellectual work well, a sort of *permanent preparation* allowing a deepening of your theological, pastoral, and spiritual meditations. It is amazing to think how the Curé of Ars, despite his exhausting days, made an effort to read every day from one of the four hundred volumes in his library!

On the other hand, it is my hope that a true sense of *fraternity* may unite you above all your differences: a sacramental and affective fraternity. *Religious priests* find support in their brothers. Secular priests experience a greater sense of solitude, and I think that the priests of the younger generations will find difficulty living alone like the Curé of Ars. Many of them are sure to find strong fraternal support and stimulation for their meditation and prayer in *priestly associations*.

Some people or lay associations are also working to help lonely and poor priests. This is highly praiseworthy.

Nonetheless, what I would like to point out is the increasingly powerful cooperation between priests and laypeople in the ministry. There is great hope for the apostolate here, and I would say it is a great incentive for priests themselves if they learn how to trust laypeople with their projects, how to discern what is best, and how to best fit into their role as priests. In this area as well, the Curé of Ars was able to stimulate the cooperation of his parishioners and make them more responsible.

13. And to you, dear *deacons*: my words this morning closely affect you, since you are members of the priestly order. Thinking of your role, I cannot help but recall the spirit of Jesus on Holy Thursday: he rose from the table, washed the feet of his disciples, and indicated service to others as the primary path to be followed at the moment of the institution of the Eucharist. *Permanent deacons*, the bishop associates you with priests through an ordination that places you forever at the service of the People of God in a way that is unique to you. The Church counts on you heavily, particularly for proclaiming the Word and catechizing, preparing the faithful for the sacraments, baptizing and distributing Holy Communion, presiding over the prayers of the community in certain circumstances, ensuring other church services, and above all bringing the witness of charity to many areas of social life. I am happy to bless you and your families.

14. At the end of this long meditation, I now return to the *missionary aspect* of our priesthood. We are called, like a good shepherd, to unite

ourselves with people wherever they are. There are many apostolic approaches to this end. It might be a discreet and patient presence communicating friendly closeness, or the sharing of living conditions and at times even work, whether in the working-class world, in the intellectual world, or in other environments that seem isolated from the Church and in need of daily and credible dialogue with a priest who is united to them in the search for a more just and fraternal world. In such cases, priests are able to exercise the ordinary ministry of their fellow pastors or chaplains.

So long as their continual spiritual reinvigoration has an apostolic motivation corresponding to a mission received from the bishop, may they know that they have the full esteem of the Church! May they always give authentic witness to the Gospel, considering it a priestly duty and preparation for more thorough evangelization! May their membership in a single, common priesthood, with which they will be interested in keeping close and frequent connections, allow them to preserve their sense of responsibility as custodians of the mysteries of Christ, and may all priests feel united by their ministry in the service of evangelization! In fact, the changes that the Gospel should evoke in society are usually the work of lay Christians in union with their priests.

It remains true, as the Curé of Ars said, that all the pastoral efforts of priests must move toward convergence on the explicit proclamation of the faith, on forgiveness, and on the Eucharist.

But above all, as Paul VI said, "never separate mission and contemplation, mission and worship, or mission and Church." Otherwise it would seem that on one side are those carrying out missionary activities with those at the margins of the Church, and on the other side are those preparing themselves for the sacraments and prayer, strengthening the Christian institution. But missionary activity is instead the work of the entire Church: it draws energy from prayer and strength from holiness.

15. In Ars, the priesthood gleamed with an entirely unique radiance. The example of St. John Mary Vianney continues to give energy to pastors throughout the world and to all priests occupied with various apostolic activities.

From this high position, in contrast with the modesty of his simple village, I give thanks to Jesus Christ for the unimaginable gift of the priesthood he has given to me, to the Curé of Ars, and to all priests past and present. They extend the holy ministry of Jesus Christ throughout the entire world, both in Christian communities and missionary outposts; they often work in difficult, clandestine, and thankless conditions for the salvation of souls and the spiritual renewal of the world that honors them at times and at other times ignores them, scorns them, and persecutes them.

I give them the homage they deserve, praying God to sustain them and reward them. And I invite the entire Christian people to join me in doing so.

I accompany my thanks with an urgent appeal to all priests: whatever your inner and outer challenges are, which the merciful Lord knows, remain faithful to your sublime vocation and to the various priestly commitments that make you men who are totally available for the service of the Gospel. In critical times, remember that no temptation to give up can be fatal before the Lord who has called you; know that you can count on the support of your brothers in the priesthood and your bishops.

The only definitive question that Jesus asks each of us, that he asks every priest, is the one he asked Peter: "Do you love me more than these?"

So then, dear brother priests, do not be afraid! If the Lord has called us to his side, he is with us through his Spirit. Let us allow ourselves to be led by the Holy Spirit as one Church.

Prayer

Lord Jesus,
as a great and unparalleled privilege,
you have made priests the ministers of God,
proclaimers of your Gospel,
and bestowers of your Body and your Word.
Fill their souls with immense enthusiasm
in the face of these sublime realities,
but also with great trust in God,
for the responsibilities and duties
you have entrusted to them are enough
to instill fear and trepidation
if the certainty of divine help does not come to their aid.
May they conform themselves to your Heart in everything they do,

may you make their ministry fruitful with goodness
and rich with merits and consolations.
May their entire lives be luminous lenses
and constant fulfillment
of their pastoral service
through humble, generous, and tireless
faith in the Gospel, in the Church,
in souls, and in their vocation.
Amen.

Thoughts By and About the Holy Curé of Ars
Humility and Obedience

From the Depths of Our Being

- "We have nothing of our own other than our will. It is the last thing we can draw upon from the depths of our being to make of it an offering to God. A single act of renouncing our will is more pleasing to him then thirty days of fasting."
- "The only sure way to please God is to remain obedient to his will in every circumstance of our lives."
- "In order to do things well, we have to do them as God wills, in full accord with his designs."
- "Just as an architect arranges the stones to construct a building, so the Lord places each of us where we are best suited."
- "What a beautiful and marvelous sight it is in the eyes of God when a religious person remains faithful to his duty and vocation!"
- "There is nothing better we can do other than obey God's will for us in everything. There we find peace, serenity, happiness, and something more: we are working for our sanctification, whereas murmuring and rebelling simply increase our guilt without remedying our condition."
- The bishop had decided to close an orphanage that was endeared to the Curé of Ars; he had decided to give the house in which it operated to a religious congregation. The lay director of the orphanage reacted in anger. "I do not see the will of the Lord in it either." The Holy Curé told her, "But the bishop does. We are left only to obey."
- When he had to receive the bishop, he prepared with fasting and penance to better understand God's will.

Joyful, Amiable, and Expansive

- "It is every day that we have to start over . . . [with] always the same reluctance."

- The idea of escaping and withdrawing continually came to mind, but that did not stop him from being just as joyful, amiable, and expansive as always, if not more.
- "We do much more for God by doing the same things without the pleasure or the appeal. It is true that every day I hoped he would send me elsewhere, but in waiting I worked as though I would never leave."
- "Every night the Lord works a little miracle for me: in the evening I can't take it anymore, and in the morning I am well-inclined."

I CAN'T TAKE IT ANYMORE

- "I have become hardened by the tedium of this wretched earth. My soul is sad to the point of death. My ears hear only painful things that rend my heart. I no longer have the time to pray. I can no longer take it."
- "I have been asking my superiors for a long time to have permission to withdraw in solitude or to a religious order of some kind."
- This servant of God had many inner sufferings. He was particularly tormented by the desire for solitude.
- "Another person would do this better than me. I desire only silence, solitude, and to be forgotten by the world."

AGAINST HIS WILL AND WITH RELUCTANCE

- "Stay where you are, this is your vocation."
- "I believe that my vocation is to be a pastor for my entire life."
- Obedience and God's will brought him back to Ars, where he remained against his will, offering God the sacrifice of that solitude he so desired.
- Every morning he had to face a great struggle . . . to resume his tiring ministry; he did so only with the greatest reluctance.
- "The Lord does not ask us for martyrdom of the body; he only asks us for martyrdom of the heart and will."

The Spiritual Temple Is Built with the Living Stones of the Holy Priesthood Shared by All the Baptized

On October 6, 1986, Pope John Paul II presided over a solemn concelebrated Mass in Ars with countless bishops and more than 3,000 priests, and he gave the following homily.

1. "He journeyed from one town and village to another" (Lk 8:1).

This is how Jesus carried out his mission as the Messiah in the Holy Land, without traveling beyond the boundaries of the nation.

This is what continues to happen whenever Jesus' disciples bring the Gospel "to the ends of the earth" (Acts 1:8). The Lord says, "I am with you" (Mt 28:20). Wherever they proclaim the Gospel, he is present.

Sometimes this presence—the saving presence of Christ—is experienced in a unique way. And at that point, a town or village acquires a particular radiance on the vast world map of evangelization.

This is precisely what happened to the town of Ars a century ago, during the years that Curé John Mary Vianney lived out his priestly ministry. Little by little, all of France and even other nations from around the world came to know the Curé of Ars. People came from all over to be near him, listen to him speak about God's love, and be healed and freed from sin. His shining example acquired new radiance after his death. Pius XI declared him the patron of pastors throughout the world. Indeed, Christ himself became uniquely present through this priest in this tiny place in France.

2. John Mary Vianney went to Ars to exercise a "holy priesthood to offer spiritual sacrifices acceptable to God through Jesus Christ" (1 Pt 2:5). He offered these sacrifices himself. Every day he offered Christ's sacrifice with such fervor: "All good works put together do not equal the sacrifice of the Mass because . . . the Holy Mass is the work of God." He invited the faithful to unite their lives to it "as a living sacrifice, holy and pleasing to God" (Rom 12:1). He offered himself: "A priest therefore does well to offer himself to God in sacrifice every morning." He offered his entire life: he was constantly united to God in prayer, worn down by serving the spiritual needs of his faithful, and secretly signed by the personal penances he took on for their conversion and salvation. He sought to imitate Christ to the utter limits of human possibility. And he became not only priest but victim, an offering like Christ.

He knew and clearly proclaimed that Jesus Christ is "a living stone" (1 Pt 2:4) and that all people—through him, with him, and in him—should also become "like living stones . . . [to] be built into a spiritual house" (1 Pt 2:5).

Dear brothers and sisters, you have countless churches in France, which are marvelous temples in which the genius of so many artists has sought in a certain sense to create—out of inert rocks—the feeling of an external space for God's presence.

John Mary Vianney blossomed as a beneficiary of the entire magnificent tradition of these temples. He himself did everything he could to beautify his little church in accordance with the style of his time so as to honor God and foster prayer in his people. Everyone knew that no external space could be this "house" that St. Peter talks about in his first letter, because none of them is in itself a "spiritual temple."

The spiritual temple must be built with the "living stones" of the holy priesthood shared by all baptized believers. And this priesthood has only one root and one source: Jesus Christ.

3. Jesus Christ! John Mary Vianney came to Ars to proclaim this fundamental truth of our faith to his parishioners: Jesus Christ, the cornerstone, chosen by God so that the temple of the eternal salvation of all mankind might be raised upon him, the temple that reunites "the entire redeemed people," the saved people.

And at the same time this is the temple of the glory of God that men and women are called to contemplate and in which they will participate according to the magnificent words of St. Irenaeus of Lyons: "The splendor of God gives life; therefore those who see God will participate in life. . . . A living man is the glory of God and the vision of God gives life to man." This faith led the Curé of Ars to say, "Our love will become the measure of the glory we will have in heaven. The love of God will fill and flood everything. . . . We will see him. . . . Jesus is everything for us. . . . All of you together form nothing other than one body with Jesus Christ."

It is true that this cornerstone—Jesus Christ—was rejected by mankind, discarded to the point of being put to death on the Cross at Golgotha; but for God he remains the "chosen and precious" stone. In fact, the scriptures say, "Behold, I am laying a stone in Zion, a cornerstone, chosen and precious, and whoever believes in it shall not be put to shame" (1 Pt 2:6).

4. John Mary Vianney came to Ars as a man who believed. He believed with his whole heart and soul, and with all the grace of his priesthood.

He believed in Christ as the cornerstone. "Whoever believes in it shall not be put to shame" (1 Pt 2:6).

The Curé of Ars brought this fundamental certainty of the faith to his parishioners: the certainty of the salvation that is in Jesus Christ.

"Therefore, its value is for you who have faith, but for those without faith: 'The stone which the builders rejected has become the cornerstone,' and 'A stone that will make people stumble, and a rock that will make them fall.' They stumble by disobeying the word" (1 Pt 2:7-8).

This is what Peter taught. This is what the Curé of Ars taught.

The word "salvation" was the one most often on the lips of John Mary Vianney. He never ceased warning his faithful—particularly the lukewarm, indifferent, sinful, and unbelieving souls—of the risk they ran for their salvation by refusing to follow the way of faith and love marked out by the Savior; he wanted to keep them from falling and becoming forever lost and removed from the Light and Love. He nevertheless added, "This good Savior is so filled with love that he seeks us everywhere." Perhaps the words of Peter and the Curé of Ars are an echo of the prophetic words that Simeon had already pronounced about the newborn Jesus, forty days after his birth: "Behold, this child is destined for the fall and rise of many in Israel, and to be a sign that will be contradicted" (Lk 2:34).

5. The Curé of Ars had the same faith in Jesus Christ that Simeon and the apostle Peter had. "There is no salvation through anyone else" (Acts 4:12).

He went to Ars strengthened by this faith, sent by the bishop to make the work of salvation present and efficacious.

His parishioners at the time were perhaps not very familiar with questions of faith, and his bishop had warned him of it: "There is not much love of God in this parish; you will bring it to them." And so it was that he did not hesitate to proclaim to these people of Ars by his words and life—and to all those who would come to join them—the message of Peter, which resounds with great power in the teachings of the Second Vatican Council: "You are 'a chosen race, a royal priesthood, a holy nation, a people of his own'" (1 Pt 2:9; see Second Vatican Council, *Lumen Gentium*, no. 9).

Yes, dear brothers and sisters, this is what you are. This is your dignity; this is your vocation as baptized and confirmed laypeople. And the reason is "'so that you may announce the praises' of him who called you out of darkness into his wonderful light" (1 Pt 2:9).

The Curé of Ars himself walked in this light. He knew it was destined for all: everyone is called to this "wonderful light."

The Second Vatican Council later emphasized this dignity and responsibility of the baptized: they participate in the priesthood of Christ by the exercise of spiritual worship, in his prophetic function by witnessing, and in his regal service. They "have received an equal privilege of faith through the justice of God" (Second Vatican Council, *Lumen Gentium*, no. 32; see 2 Pt 1:1) and "the chosen People of God is one. . . . As members, they share a common dignity from their rebirth in Christ. They have the same filial grace and the same vocation to perfection" (Second Vatican Council, *Lumen Gentium*, no. 32). The Curé of Ars never ceased reminding his faithful of their dignity as beings loved by God, sanctified by Christ, and called to follow him.

6. Yes, we are all called—and constantly called—to come to the light and come out of the darkness. At times it may be a very profound darkness, a darkness that enshrouds the spirit: the darkness of sin and the darkness of unbelief.

One hundred years later, the Second Vatican Council would be faced with the same reality. It would risk the path of encounter and dialogue with nonbelievers and believers of other religions, all while knowing that we are always and definitively dealing with a question of the "dialogue of salvation," as my predecessor Paul VI so aptly defined it.

The Curé of Ars also knew very well that the dialogue of salvation is what is important, and he constantly promoted it with all the means available to him at his time. Can we possibly reproach him for having conducted this dialogue of salvation in such simple and bare places that are still so moving to us? Can we upbraid him for working from this old catechist's desk and in the confessional that he so tirelessly kept occupied?

7. What counts is that first of all there was a true dialogue of salvation, an extraordinarily fruitful dialogue that leaves us perplexed even today.

The fruits it brought were due to this "wonderful light" that comes not from man, but from God. The priestly ministry of forgiveness is always a gift from on high: through the priest who has been ordered to this ministry, it is Christ who enlightens, heals, and forgives. The burning love of the Curé of Ars lent itself splendidly to this work of Christ.

The fruits it brought were fruits of mercy: the merciful love of God, thanks to which those who "had not received mercy" came back having "received mercy" (see 1 Pt 2:10). They came back converted. They came back absolved from their sins.

The Curé of Ars attributed these words to Christ: "I will charge my ministers with letting them know I am always ready to receive them, for my mercy is infinite."

O dear brothers and sisters, do you give sufficient weight to the incredible grace there is in being absolved of your sins, returning to God's love and a state of friendship with him, being filled with him, being reborn into the Life of God, and being reincorporated into the people sanctified by God? Do you look to the Cross on which Christ gave his own life for this Redemption? Do you desire this forgiveness and this spiritual rebirth that we cannot give to ourselves and without which our communion with God and neighbor is not real? Do you seriously prepare yourselves for it? Do you ask this Sacrament of Reconciliation of your priests? Do you live and celebrate it properly?

Thanks to the humble service of the Curé of Ars, those who were "no people" truly became "God's people" (see 1 Pt 2:10): the temple made of living stones and built upon the cornerstone of Christ (see 1 Pt 2:4-6).

8. Building the Church! This is what the Curé of Ars did in his village. Prepared by his rough and simple preaching, conversion and forgiveness would allow his parishioners to advance in the union of their lives to God, in Christian conduct, in witness, and in apostolic responsibility.

The Eucharist was the climax of the parish gatherings. He celebrated in such a way that each person became vividly aware of the presence of Christ. He encouraged those who were properly prepared to receive Communion frequently.

He taught his parishioners to pray and to adore the Blessed Sacrament; or rather, they felt themselves drawn to come pray with him in the church.

He took care to ensure that no work or commitment would conflict with the Sunday celebration. Running the risk of enduring calumnies from those who opposed him, in his homilies he fought the customs and habits he saw to be contrary to the spirit of truth, honesty, purity, and charity of the Gospel, while promoting healthy local festivities.

His parish quickly took on a new aspect. He himself never missed an opportunity to visit the sick and their families. He was particularly concerned for the poor, the orphans, and the uneducated children. He gathered the youth and strengthened family fathers and mothers in terms of their educational responsibilities. He established confraternities and elicited the aid of parishioners who took on the responsibilities of certain activities. He surrounded himself with assistants whom he had educated, and he started up popular missions. He educated the people in prayer and missionary aid at a time when another son of this diocese, St. Peter Chanel, was leaving for Oceania and died as a martyr on Futuna Island.

And so the Curé of Ars encouraged the various vocations of service to the Church in accordance with the means, methods, and needs of his time. Together with the laypeople and in communion with his fellow priests, his bishop, and the pope, he built a temple of God in this place.

But everyone knew the extent to which his irreplaceable ministry of the priesthood—fulfilled in the name of Jesus Christ, with the Holy Spirit—had sparked, energized, and fueled this progress.

9. So it was that Christ truly came to be present here, in Ars, during the time that John Mary Vianney was pastor.

Yes, he came to be present indeed. He saw "the crowds" of men and women during that time "troubled and abandoned, like sheep without a shepherd" (Mt 9:36).

Christ came to be present here as the Good Shepherd. "A good shepherd, a pastor pleasing to God's heart," John Mary Vianney said, "is the greatest treasure the Good Lord can grant to a parish, and one of the most precious gifts of divine mercy."

In this place, Christ spoke to his disciples and to the whole Church in France and throughout the world as he once did in Palestine: "The harvest is abundant but the laborers are few; so ask the master of the harvest to send out laborers for his harvest" (Lk 10:2).

Today he is telling us the same thing, because the needs are vast and urgent. The bishops, successors of the Apostles, and the Successor of Peter see the vastness of the harvest more than most, along with the promises of renewal, as well as the misery of so many souls left unaided, with few apostolic laborers.

Priests have a vivid awareness of this need: they see their ranks thinning in many places, and they await the commitment of more young people to the priesthood and religious life.

The laity in general and families are equally sure of this need: they count on the priestly ministry to nourish their faith and encourage their apostolic life.

Children and young people know it well: they need priests to become disciples of Jesus, and perhaps even to share in the joy that comes from consecrating oneself entirely to the service of the Lord for his harvest.

And all of us who are gathered here, after having meditated on the life and service of John Mary Vianney, the Curé of Ars, this unique "laborer" of the harvest in which the salvation of mankind is accomplished, raise our fervent petition to the Master of the harvest, praying for the Church throughout the world, "Send laborers for your harvest! Send laborers!"

The Missionary Identity of Priests in the Church, as an Intrinsic Aspect of the Exercise of the *Tria Munera*

On March 16, 2009, Pope Benedict XVI received in an audience the members of the Congregation for the Clergy on the occasion of their plenary assembly. He gave them a speech on the missionary identity of the priesthood and announced his intention to inaugurate a Year for Priests to run from June 19, 2009, to June 19, 2010, in association with the 150th anniversary of the death of the Holy Curé of Ars.

Your Eminences,
Venerable Brothers in the Episcopate and in the Priesthood,
I am glad to be able to welcome you at a special Audience on the eve of my departure for Africa, where I am going to present the *Instrumentum Laboris* of the Second Special Assembly of the Synod for Africa that will be held here in Rome next October. I thank Cardinal Cláudio Hummes for the kind words with which he has interpreted the sentiments you share and I thank you for the beautiful letter you wrote to me. With him, I greet you all, Superiors, Officials and Members of the Congregation, with gratitude for all the work you do at the service of such an important sector of the Church's life.

Pope Benedict XVI, Address to the members of the Congregation for the Clergy (March 16, 2009), *www.vatican.va/holy_father/benedict_xvi/speeches/2009/march/documents/ hf_ben-xvi_spe_20090316_plenaria-clero_en.html.*

The theme you have chosen for this Plenary Assembly, "The missionary identity of the priest in the Church as an intrinsic dimension of the exercise of the *tria munera*," suggests some reflections on the work of these days and the abundant fruit that it will certainly yield. If the whole Church is missionary and if every Christian, by virtue of Baptism and Confirmation *quasi ex officio* (cf. *Catechism of the Catholic Church*, no. 1305), receives the mandate to profess the faith publicly, the ministerial priesthood, also from this viewpoint, is ontologically distinct, and not only by rank, from the baptismal priesthood that is also known as the "common priesthood." In fact, the apostolic mandate "Go into all the world and preach the Gospel to the whole of creation" (Mk 16:15) is constitutive of the ministerial priesthood. This mandate is not, as we know, a mere duty entrusted to collaborators; its roots are deeper and must be sought further back in time.

The missionary dimension of the priesthood is born from the priest's sacramental configuration to Christ. As a consequence it brings with it a heartfelt and total adherence to what the ecclesial tradition has identified as *apostolica vivendi forma*. This consists in participation in a "new life," spiritually speaking, in that "new way of life" which the Lord Jesus inaugurated and which the Apostles made their own. Through the imposition of the Bishop's hands and the consecratory prayer of the Church, the candidates become new men, they become "presbyters." In this light it is clear that the *tria munera* are first a gift and only consequently an office, first a participation in a life, and hence a *potestas*. Of course, the great ecclesial tradition has rightly separated sacramental efficacy from the concrete existential situation of the individual priest and so the legitimate expectations of the faithful are appropriately safeguarded. However, this correct doctrinal explanation takes nothing from the necessary, indeed indispensable, aspiration to moral perfection that must dwell in every authentically priestly heart.

Precisely to encourage priests in this striving for spiritual perfection on which, above all, the effectiveness of their ministry depends, I have decided to establish a special "Year for Priests" that will begin on June 19 [in 2009] and last until June 19, 2010. In fact, it is the 150th anniversary of the death of the Holy Curé of Ars, John Mary Vianney, who is a true example of a pastor at the service of Christ's flock. It will be the task of your Congregation, in agreement with the diocesan Ordinaries and with the superiors of religious institutes, to promote and to coordinate the various spiritual and pastoral initiatives that seem useful for making the importance of the priest's role and mission in the Church and in contemporary society ever more clearly perceived.

The priest's mission, as the theme of the Plenary Assembly emphasizes, is carried out "in the Church." This ecclesial, communal, hierarchical and doctrinal dimension is absolutely indispensable to every authentic mission and, alone guarantees its spiritual effectiveness. The four aspects mentioned must always be recognized as intimately connected: the mission is "ecclesial" because no one proclaims himself in the first person, but within and through his own humanity every priest must be well aware that he is bringing to the world Another, God himself. God is the only treasure which ultimately people desire to find in a priest. The mission is "communal" because it is carried out in a unity and communion that only secondly has also important aspects of social visibility. Moreover, these derive essentially from that divine intimacy in which the priest is called to be expert, so that he may be able to lead the souls entrusted to him humbly and trustingly to the same encounter with the Lord. Lastly, the "hierarchical" and "doctrinal" dimensions suggest reaffirming the importance of the ecclesiastical discipline (the term has a connection with "disciple") and doctrinal training and not only theological, initial and continuing formation.

Awareness of the radical social changes that have occurred in recent decades must motivate the best ecclesial forces to supervise the formation of candidates for the ministry. In particular, it must foster the constant concern of Pastors for their principal collaborators, both by cultivating truly fatherly human relations and by taking an interest in their continuing formation, especially from the doctrinal and spiritual viewpoints. The mission is rooted in a special way in a good formation, developed in communion with uninterrupted ecclesial Tradition, without breaks or temptations of irregularity. In this sense, it is important to encourage in priests, especially in the young generations, a correct reception of the texts of the Second Ecumenical Vatican Council, interpreted in the light of the Church's entire fund of doctrine. It seems urgent to recover that awareness that has always been at the heart of the Church's mission, which impels priests to be present, identifiable and recognizable both for their judgment of faith, for their personal virtues as well as for the habit, in the contexts of culture and of charity.

As Church and as priests, we proclaim Jesus of Nazareth Lord and Christ, Crucified and Risen, Sovereign of time and of history, in the glad certainty that this truth coincides with the deepest expectations of the human heart. In the mystery of the Incarnation of the Word, that is, of the fact that God became man like us, lies both the content and the method of Christian proclamation. The true dynamic center of the mission is here: in Jesus Christ, precisely. The centrality of Christ brings with it the correct appreciation of the ministerial priesthood, without which there would be neither the Eucharist, nor even the mission nor the Church herself. In this regard it is necessary to be alert to ensure that the "new structures" or pastoral organizations are not planned on the basis of an erroneous interpretation of the proper promotion of the laity for a time in which one would have "to do without" the ordained ministry, because in that case the presuppositions for a further dilution of the ministerial priesthood would be laid and possible presumed "solutions" might come dramatically to coincide with the real causes of contemporary problems linked to the ministry.

I am certain that in these days the work of the Plenary Assembly, under the protection of the *Mater Ecclesiae*, will be able to examine these brief ideas that I permit myself to submit to the attention of the Cardinals, Archbishops and Bishops, while I invoke upon you all an abundance of heavenly gifts, as a pledge of which I impart a special, affectionate Apostolic Blessing to you and to all your loved ones.

The Patron of Pastors

It is difficult to imagine a life any simpler and any more lacking in major outside events than that of John Mary Vianney, the Holy Curé of Ars.

The distance is very short from the village where he was born in 1786 to the one that made him immortal, yet it was almost the only trip he ever took. For forty years he wanted to be only the pastor of Ars.

And this reminds us that *today, just like in the past, people are won over not by striking words but by stunning example.*

The pilgrimages to Ars, which began while the saint was still alive, are one of the greatest religious occurrences in that, unlike other pilgrimages evoked by apparitions and miracles, they were essentially sparked by the personage of this holy priest, who seemed to attract souls from his place inside the confessional.

For years and years, whole caravans of penitents (an average of eighty thousand each year) would set out, and people living in a time period thought to be anything but inclined to such enthusiasms were left enchanted by such evident holiness.

The importance of the Curé of Ars is to be recognized more in the testimony of his presence alone than in his teachings and the way they were expressed.

He was a saint recognized as such by an entire people while he was still alive: this is a phenomenon that might have been thought ancient or medieval, but it was instead made evidently manifest in an age so close to our own.

That little priest with a pallid and angular countenance, whose bashfulness betrayed his country roots, radiated an extraordinary light. The portraits we have of him allow us to imagine a bit: that gaze and that smile have something supernatural to them.

He had only just passed (in 1859), but the people already wished to see him remembered next to the altars. In fact, there is no French church today that does not have a statue of the old priest wearing his surplice and stole, still so moving despite such a conventional style.

This is precisely how we should imagine the Curé of Ars: a priest forever. The elevated mysticism often flowing from the silence of cloisters arose in him from his mission as a countryside pastor, and specifically from the faithful fulfillment of it, which is ultimately the same mission of every shepherd of souls: thus he attained the heights of mystical union.

His story, while not boasting any earth-shattering events, is a marvelous one. *He was an extraordinary man in ordinary things.*

A young priest was sent to a parish where faith was dead. By word and example he kneaded that human dough, fermented it, and transformed it. His entire apostolate was rich with merits.

He had an infallible psychological sureness, boundless dedication, and above all that love of souls without which one can be neither a priest nor a Christian.

He fulfilled two of the essential tasks of the priesthood with true greatness: preaching ("he preached with his entire self," and all witnesses unanimously agreed on the power of his simple words, which move us still today even though they were taken from unoriginal texts at times); and the ministry of confession, which became increasingly arduous as his fame grew.

It is difficult to imagine the suffering it must have caused him during long periods in the confessional in which he had to offer endless responses to questions, advice, and consolation from the morning hours until eight or nine o'clock at night.

In order to better understand the experience of the Curé of Ars, we need to look to more modern examples like St. Leopold Mandić and St. Pio of Pietrelcina.

In his writings about the priesthood, the Curé of Ars says that one is a priest not for himself but for others. He lived this truth, and—like the hero in Manuel Gálvez's *Jueves Santo*—he died exhausted by the fatigue sustained in the confessional.

If there has been anyone who has proven that the "ordinary" Christian and the mystic do not differ in essence but only in degree on the scales of heaven, it was precisely this poor village pastor who touched God by drawing on the ordinary priestly virtues.

We can attribute less importance to all the rest, which is to say to all the extraordinary things that accompanied his life. The fact that the Curé of Ars may have been a miracle worker and that many witnesses describe him as a clairvoyant who often predicted the future and foresaw certain events are simply "flowerets" or supplemental signs.

He was undoubtedly privileged with moments of ecstasy, and he often spoke of the terrible struggles he had to endure against the powers of evil, specifically against the one he expressively referred to as "the claw."

There was such an evident supernatural atmosphere surrounding him that even the most irrational occurrences became more explainable.

He was a man who lived in the world where his charity appeared, and at the same time in another world where it was impossible to follow him. They are truly the "alternatives of heaven and hell."

One of his successors at the parish of Ars who carefully studied his works, Msgr. Convert, says that his writings often give the impression of being inspired by the Holy Spirit even in their simplicity, and so the myth of the Holy Curé's intellectual poverty should be discarded.

It is also certain that he had mystical experiences, though his humility kept him from delving into any description, because every once in a while an allusion would slip out. An example is what he wrote about the annihilation of the soul, which gives us reason to believe that he too was one of the priests who truly saw Jesus on the altar.

Humility and discretion: these are the two words that should always be repeated when talking about the Curé of Ars.

He did not allow his prodigious life to be enticed by pride for even a moment. He preserved this total humility even in the almost incredible penances he took on, almost as if to indicate that everything he did was entirely natural.

The supernatural love he harbored for the crosses he willingly bore on his shoulders radiated all around him. One of his biographers, Fr. Monnin, said that this holiness had become second nature to him toward the end of his life—but it is not hard to imagine the price he must have paid in sacrifice.

The way he treated his body, which he called "the old Adam" or his "corpse," might be surprising and even shocking if we did not know that everything was sublimated by his love and transfigured by his serene smile.

If anyone was able to reconcile or unite both the mystic and the ascetic in himself, it was surely the Curé of Ars, who always considered the most challenging trials not as ends in themselves but as heroic means of reaching the transcendent.

Is it proper to talk about a "doctrine" of the Curé of Ars? At a certain point on the scale of mystical experience, there are no longer just the relationships between the soul and the created world that expand and contract, but also those of the intellect and the realm of ideas.

Everything we know about the Curé of Ars confirms the presence of an elevated spirituality formulated into the humble language of the people. His examples were not always perfectly fitting, but they were always striking and incisive.

To help his listeners understand how impurity leaves an indelible mark on the soul, he compared it to an oil stain on a piece of wool: even if the cloth is washed ten times, the stain does not come out.

His whole style abounds with descriptive visual terms. His works can be summed up as simple homilies written in many different ways or as the catecheses he explained to his parishioners without much original thought, since we could say that he sought only to teach the fundamental truths of the faith.

The dominant aspects of his thinking are the most traditional concepts of Christianity: abandonment of the soul to God, love of God, acceptance of suffering, and offering one's entire life to Divine Providence.

If we wanted to identify the core of his "doctrine," we would do well to recall his worship of the Eucharist; but even in this case, his words say nothing new: their greatness comes from the intensity of his feeling and his total submission to the divine law.

Should we then deduce from this intellectual humility that the Curé of Ars was ignorant? It has been said all too many times, and some have even affirmed that it was precisely because of his ignorance that he came to be honored around the altars.

This is one of the many errors our reason commits when it attempts to understand humankind outside of the proper hierarchy in which the value of intelligence is not the most important one.

St. Paul writes, "God chose the foolish of the world to shame the wise, and God chose the weak of the world to shame the strong, and God chose the lowly and despised of the world, those who count for nothing, to reduce to nothing those who are something, so that no human being might boast before God" (1 Cor 1:27-29).

Yet as Fr. Monnin rightly pointed out, while it is wrong to consider John Mary Vianney ignorant, it is nonetheless true that he was not cut out well for studies. But this was not a unique case. Pope John Paul I would often say with disarming simplicity during the Angelus in St. Peter's Square, "If I had known I was going to be pope one day, oh, how much more I would have studied!"

In the case of the Curé of Ars, it is essential to understand the barrier that separates the most educated person or the best trained theologian from what surpasses all study and all theology: absolute union with God.

Bishop Belley admirably highlighted this difference one day in his response to various priests who were criticizing the Curé's ignorance and lack of preparation in casuistry: "I do not know if he is educated, but he is certainly inspired!"

The world of the saints is a world of wonder. And everything in the life of the Curé of Ars is one continuous wonder.

It is pointless to seek new ways of thinking in him; instead, we will find new ways of working in him. His claim to perfect holiness, so to speak, is not uniqueness but normality.

This saint is a saint not because he is so extraordinary and therefore inimitable, but because of his perfection and constancy in observing the law that should be common to the entire Christian people.

In this way, all priests—particularly those involved in active pastoral service—can *feel* this model of holiness closer to themselves, feel drawn to an example of holiness that is neither abstract nor generic, and follow that same lifestyle in order to become priests in conformity with the heart of Jesus.